SAINT THOMAS AQUINAS A BIOGRAPHY FOR YOUNG READERS

*BY MARY ELLEN EVANS,
GEOFFREY GNEUHS AND MARGARET NICHOLS*

NEW PRIORY PRESS

EXPLORING THE DOMINICAN VISION

Table of Contents

Table of Illustrations

Figure 1   Boy Thomas: noble family, Monte Cassino, Learning

Chapter 1: "What is God?"

The Will of God

"Nana!"

Thomas was sitting straight up on his small bed and screaming. The lightning, which had been clawing the sky beyond the thick walls of Roccasecca Castle, had come inside the nursery and struck with a hissing sound. There was a deafening clap of thunder; then the wind and rain stopped, and everything was quiet. Everything, that is, except Thomas.

Nana glided over to his bed, picked up the candle from his nightstand, and peered down at the screaming child. "Thank God, you're safe," she said. "Cover up now and go back to sleep like a good boy. It's only the first storm of spring." Then she glided over to the other cot.

Thomas was far from sleep by now. He stood up on his bed, shivering in the cold, to see Nana peering down into his baby sister's crib.

"Holy Mother of God!" cried the young nurse. Then she set down her candle, picked up the baby girl, breathed frantically into her mouth, laid her down again, and ran wildly out of the room.

Thomas climbed out of his high bed and stole over to look at tiny Maria. By the candle glow she looked stiff, and her eyes were wide open, just like one of his big sisters' dolls. He was just about to pat her head, the way small big brothers show how they love their baby sisters, when Nana rushed in with the Countess Theodora.

"She's dead, my lady, she's dead," Nana kept sobbing.

Countess Theodora picked up her baby, clasped her to her breast, and looked up beyond the high casement windows. Thomas figured that his mother was praying, for Nana had made a quick Sign of the Cross and bowed her head. But then, noticing Thomas on the cold floor at their side, Nana swooped down like a falcon, carried him back to his bed, and covered him up over his ears—all without a word.

Thomas was too much surprised and puzzled to make a sound, and he even forgot to ask any of the questions a wide-awake four-year-old is forever asking—and that was most unusual for him. But he didn't intend to miss anything. He pulled the thick goose-feather comforters down just enough so that he could see what was going on without freezing his nose.

His mother, who had been standing there motionless, turned away a bit unsteadily toward the big oaken door with Maria in her arms, and Nana was instantly at her side. She put her strong right arm around Countess Theodora's waist and gently led her out.

"It's God's way, my lady. God wanted her—and you have six more," Nana was saying. " 'Tis the will of God."

"Yes, Nana," Countess Theodora echoed, "it is the will of God."

Just as they got to the door, Thomas stuck his whole head out of the covers and called after her, "Mother, what is God?" His mother seemed not to have heard, but Nana turned back and said in a fierce whisper, "Hush you, Thomas, and go to sleep."

If Nana had known such a big word, she might have added, "This is no time for theology." But Nana was only a brown-eyed, great-hearted peasant girl who had never gone to school and had learned everything she knew right at Roccasecca Castle, where she had been born and brought up, like her mother and father before her.

Castle Life

But somehow things were never quite the same for Thomas after that night. Up until now he had lived a carefree, happy-go-lucky life and enjoyed every minute of it. His was a small boy's world full of all sorts of delightful things. There were always dogs to trot around after you, and birds you couldn't quite catch, and flowers growing luxuriantly in the castle flower beds; and Nana's father sometimes let Thomas help him with his gardening, showing him how to plant and hoe and trim.

There was the armory full of swords and lances and spears and coats-of-mail, and a red-hot forge where the blacksmith hammered away, stripped to his waist—and where a small boy was very much in the way. There were sewing rooms where Countess Theodora and her daughters and maids-in-waiting sat at the looms and wove and made lovely designs as they chatted. Also, stables and smoke house and bake house and the big stone kitchen with its heavenly smells and heart-breaking sights—like when a little pig who had been one's friend was now roasting on the spit—and always the possibility that the cook had slyly made a special little tart for a special small boy.

Moreover, there were such interesting people: the swarthy laborers who smiled at the junior-grade nobleman, and the very tall castle guards who could hardly bend low enough to see him, and the rather terrifying big brothers who were almost never home at the same time, what with schooling and jousting and then going off to the wars with their father and Emperor Frederick. There were also his older sisters who petted him and teased him between trips to Naples and neighboring castles on strictly feminine business.

Sometimes a wandering trader, his pack horse almost sagging in two with merchandise, would be allowed over the drawbridge into the courtyard. And there, before Thomas's popping eyes, he would undo his sacks of silks and spices and jewels and goblets and finely tooled leather and richly dyed rugs from the Orient. And if the trader was well mannered, Countess Theodora might invite him to the family fire after he had been fed, so that he could give them all the latest news—for they had no newspapers or television in the thirteenth century.

Sometimes it might be a wandering hermit, looking for hospitality for the night in exchange for prayers, or Gypsies—those brown-skinned, black-eyed, ear-ringed people from nobody-knew-where —who sang and danced and fiddled until you thought they would drop, for the price of a meal and some old clothing to wear on top of their rags.

And there was the castle itself, with its four great white towers frowning down on the valleys and their blue slate steeples so high that they scratched at the sky (or so it seemed to four-year-old Thomas), and the little towers inside the courtyard—not much taller, some of them, than the coifs the ladies wore. And all the nooks and crannies and hiding places and stairs and galleries and the slits of windows, which his father had glass put in to please his bride, who had come from far up north in Europe, and which gave Thomas a peephole onto the vast world beyond Roccasecca.

Up to now, there was world enough to satisfy any small boy right in his own castle, and Thomas was so busy taking everything in that it never occurred to him that things were not always just as nice as they seemed. But after that night when lightning had killed his little sister, and Nana had said that God did it, Thomas began to grow up. He seemed to do less tasting and smelling and feeling, and more thinking. Maybe he was getting a bit too serious for one so young, but he had a big worry on his mind. If God allowed the lightning that killed his sister, how could He be the same God who had made the stars and the flowers and all the people Thomas loved? Maybe Thomas was just getting the use of reason.

At any rate, when Count Landolph suddenly came home from the wars, he discovered that Thomas was a baby no longer. He was now five years old, a big boy for his age, too, with fair hair like his Norman ancestors, a tawny-wheaty color to his fair skin, and the gentlest, deepest expression in his clear, wondering eyes. Not a day too soon to start training him for his future! No Aquino as big as Thomas should be left to dream and mope about like this! Count Landolph was a knight-warrior, and he expected all his sons to be knight-warriors, too. Now that he had some time on his hands, he was going to initiate Thomas personally.

"Thomas," he announced one fine morning in 1229, as he found the boy sitting on a stone step watching a brood of new kittens having their breakfast, "today I'm going to teach you how to hunt. Come, up with you!" Count Landolph was already on his way.

"You mean with a falcon, Father?" asked Thomas as he scrambled to his feet and trotted after him, three steps to his father's one.

"Yes. With my blue falcon, in fact."

Now, although Thomas was not very much interested in learning how to hunt, it would not have occurred to him to disobey his father. Besides, he did want to see the famous blue falcon, a large, fierce-eyed, hawk-like bird, for God had made it, and just now Thomas was interested in anything God had made. So he dutifully followed his father to the stables where Count Landolph kept his falcons. Thomas watched him draw on a long leather glove, and heard him explain that if he did not take this precaution, the falcon's claws might cut into his sleeve or even into his arm.

After the bird was perching securely on his father's arm, they left by the castle gates and climbed wordlessly into the wooded hills beyond. When they had reached a clearing, his father stopped walking, and Thomas panted up beside him. "Now," Count Landolph began, "we'll see what this bird can do."

In spite of himself, Thomas watched intently. The shining eye of the falcon was alert—something must have been moving in the thick underbrush. Then the bird flew off its perch and circled over some bushes. It swooped down into the grass. In another second it was flying back to Count Landolph's arm, carrying a lifeless, bleeding rabbit in its beak. The count threw the rabbit to the ground and fed the falcon with some breadcrumbs from his pocket.

"A good bird, Thomas," his father observed. "Would you like a falcon for yourself?"

"N-n-no, Father," Thomas replied.

Count Landolph straightened up in surprise and said, "And why not?" He was beginning to be displeased. His tall figure stood over Thomas.

"Because, uh, I think it is, well, uh, because God made that little rabbit and, uh—"

Count Landolph didn't let him finish. This was just too much. What kind of soldier would this soft-hearted child make? He whisked around and started back down the hill. Thomas, throwing a forlorn look at the little rabbit, followed him.

As they entered the castle yard, Ronald and Landolph Jr., Thomas's next-oldest brothers, who had come home with their father, were mounted on their horses at opposite ends of the yard. They held their reins in their left hands, and their lances, straight-up, in their right hands. They were wearing armor and heavy helmets covered their faces. The points of their lances were tipped for protection, as they were only practicing.

"Go!" Count Landolph shouted, as he stopped to watch them begin their play-joust. He even forgot about Thomas for a moment, and his precious falcon flew back to the roost on its own initiative.

The two brothers spurred their horses and galloped fiercely forward. Thomas was sure that they would pierce each other, coming on with such force and speed. But young Landolph managed to shift in his saddle and avoid Ronald's thrust. Then he spun his horse about and caught Ronald with a heavy jab. Ronald was so shaken by the blow that he dropped his lance. It clattered on the cobblestones above the noise of the horses' hooves. His brother then rode after him and pushed him off his horse.

Thomas seized his father's hand. "They'll kill each other," he said in horror.

"It's either kill or be killed in warfare, son," his father answered gently. Then he shouted, "Good work, Landolph. And Ronald, a little less dreaming and a little more concentration and you'll make the grade."

"But why do men have to kill each other?" Thomas persisted.

"You ask too many questions, Thomas. When you get a little older, you'll understand. Just remember that there never was an Aquino who did not go forth to battle. You are a cousin of the Holy Roman Emperor. All the Aquinos have served him well, and you will, too."

"I don't want to, Father," said Thomas, shaken by his own bluntness.

Count Landolph was annoyed all over again. "Thomas, I don't know what to say to you. Come, we'll have to have a talk with your mother." And he took Thomas's hand and fairly lifted him along to the great hall of the castle.

Thomas hardly had time to be worried, but he did realize that, for the first time he could remember, he was in disgrace. He must have been very wicked if he had upset his father like this; yet he knew inside that all he had done was tell the truth.

His father tossed him up on his shoulder and took the stone stairs at a fast clip. Then he burst in with his load and dumped it at his wife's feet. Countess Theodora had just got up from her prie-dieu, and now seated herself very regally and picked up her embroidery. That was the best way of calming down her husband, she had found.

Count Landolph strode back and forth across the floor, then stopped in his tracks. "Theodora," he thundered, "I don't know what to do with this son of yours."

"Now, Landolph," she said quietly, "what has he done?"

"It isn't what he's done, it's what he won't do . . . I don't think we'll ever make a soldier out of him. All he does is talk about God. Guess he's been around you womenfolk too much."

"But, Landolph, he doesn't have to be a soldier. He could be a Benedictine monk. Would you like to be a Benedictine, Thomas?"

"I don't know what that is, but if I could be a good one, Mother—"

"You see, Landolph? A good monk . . . abbot of Monte Cassino . . . I have just been waiting for you to come home to ask you; it really is time we began his schooling. He seems young to us but he is growing up so fast, and with your uncle Sinebald as lord abbot . . ."

"You think that Uncle Sinebald would have him after all the . . ."

Countess Theodora put her finger to her lip. Then she said, "Of course he would, Landolph! It might be a sort of peace-offering, and Thomas will be lord abbot someday." She smiled at the idea.

Count Landolph rubbed his hands together in satisfaction. "Exactly!" he beamed. "I should have thought of that myself."

Monte Cassino

Neither Thomas nor his father was enjoying this trip to Monte Cassino very much. At first, Thomas had been all excited at the prospect of going away to school and learning so many things, but when the time had come to say good-bye to Roccasecca and all his pets and friends and his mother and sisters and Nana, he began to wonder if it was worth it. And now that they were almost there, he began to get really frightened.

And his father—well, he dreaded facing Uncle Sinebald. He had a very bad conscience, after what Emperor Frederick II had done to the monks, and he wasn't at all sure that the monks would be very glad to see him or train his youngest son to be their lord abbot. On the other hand, he was an Aquino, and he had power, and he could threaten the monks with even worse things than had happened if they didn't cooperate. All this was lost on Thomas, of course. He hadn't understood what his mother and father were saying that day of the big decision, but he had caught that quick gesture of his mother's, which made his father stop saying whatever he was going to say.

Thomas sat erect, with his father's left arm holding him tightly as he guided the horse with his right. Trailing behind was the count's henchman watching for bandits and leading a small pack horse that carried Thomas's extra clothes. First, there was the long climb down the paths from Roccasecca to the village of Aquino and the valley, then the long, twisting climb up the far side of another mountain while the hot August sun blazed down on them. It was only about eight miles altogether, but it seemed more like eight hundred to both of them.

Suddenly, the great abbey loomed into sight, and they forgot everything else for it was so beautiful. For more than seven hundred years it had stood on that mountain, above the ruins of a pagan temple to Apollo, and thousands of monks had lived and died within its walls. Thomas had never seen a monk, but he began to feel very curious about them.

Abbot Sinebald kept them waiting just the right length of time: not too long, as that would have been discourteous; not too short, as that might have been too courteous to a man (and his nephew at that) who had helped Emperor Frederick destroy the old abbey, kill the monks, set fire to their crops, and steal their beautiful altar vessels. Then Count Landolph was motioned in to the abbot's room by the tall young man in black robes who had received them first. When Thomas started in after his father, the young man grasped him lightly by the shoulder. "No, boy, you stay outside with me."

"But that's Granduncle Sinebald!" Thomas protested. "Why can't—"

"Why can't you go right in with your father? Because sometimes grown-ups have matters to discuss that little boys would not understand."

At length the big door opened, and Count Landolph stepped out, looking as though he had recently been angry but was all over it now; he was followed by the lord abbot. The young monk, and his new young friend who had been pacing up and down the corridor, came to attention as the lord abbot said, "So this is little Thomas Aquinas?"

"Thomas Aquinas it is, Your Lordship," the monk answered as he pushed Thomas ahead of him for the abbot's very grown-up handshake. Count Landolph smiled down on his small son. Thomas was too overcome for words, but the abbot went on, "Well, now, your father tells me that you have a head for learning. If that is true, this is the place for you. And I appoint Dom Cuthbert here," he nodded to the younger monk, "to take full charge of you."

Thomas looked up timidly at Dom Cuthbert but was reassured by his friendly look. His father meanwhile was growing impatient: he wanted to get back to Roccasecca before nightfall. He made his farewells to the abbot and Dom Cuthbert, then knelt to Thomas's level, kissed him tenderly, and off he went. The abbot returned to his office.

Thomas had a moment of desolation and might even have cried, but then he felt Dom Cuthbert's calm blue eyes upon him. Thomas looked up at him, full of trust, and said, "Please, Dom Cuthbert, could you tell me about God?"

Chapter 2: School Daze

Abbey Studies

Thomas was in a daze. He had never expected that school would be like this. It must be the biggest place in all the world—or so it seemed as he trudged along with Dom Cuthbert, his eyes popping in the effort not to miss a thing that his guide was pointing out to him. For Thomas was having the "grand tour" of the great old abbey on his first afternoon at school.

First they went to the abbey church, which looked as big as the cathedral of Naples, or anyway a million times bigger than the tiny oratory at home. And—wonder of wonders—God was right there, so Dom Cuthbert said, inside His house on the altar. Thomas made a mental note to ask Dom Cuthbert more about this later. If God was right here, then all his questions would soon be answered.

Then they had a peek at the scriptorium, where the monks on their high stools were writing laboriously, hardly looking up when Dom Cuthbert and his small charge stole in, for fear they might lose their place in the manuscripts they were copying. Then that wonderful place called the library, lined with shelves that were crammed with scrolls and bound parchments full of words. Then the weaving and carpentry and tool shops, and ever so much more—it was all so fascinating.

And somewhere along the way—for it was a warm September day and they had walked a thousand miles (so Thomas thought)—they landed in the kitchen, and Thomas was suddenly hoisted upon a stool at a fat oak worktable alongside a knotted-up but smiling old monk who was peeling potatoes by the bushel. A beaker of cool fresh milk and a slab of warm brown bread appeared before Thomas as if by magic. No one said a word, but the monk at the baking ovens and the monk at the hearth and the monk at the pots and pans all turned around from their work to smile, like the turnip peeler, at the little newcomer.

After some sightseeing they returned to their starting point just as a great bell boomed out from somewhere. Dom Cuthbert pulled his new student out of the way as a horde of boys of all shapes and sizes trooped into the corridor to line up for supper in their refectory. All afternoon there hadn't been a boy in sight, and Thomas could only hear their scuffling noises and the murmur of voices coming out of closed classroom doors, and then the shouting and screaming from some remote part of the grounds as they played their games after school. Now Dom Cuthbert led Thomas to the refectory after them. He found him a place at the end of the table that was almost as long as the room—and the room was as long as the chapel (in fact, it was right under it). Thomas felt a thousand eyes upon him, and he wished he were anywhere but there.

Dom Cuthbert wedged him in between the two last boys, whom he introduced as Pietro Orsini and Giovanni Caetani. As a lay brother came along with a huge steaming kettle and started ladling out some wonderful-smelling broth into the wooden bowls lined far down the table, Dom Cuthbert wandered over to the window to inspect a rose vine that was creeping over the sill. And in that instant Pietro slyly reached over for Thomas's bowl of soup and emptied it into his own. Before Thomas had time to react (and you may be sure he was hungry again by now), Dom Cuthbert was on the spot. He reached over Pietro's shoulder and emptied the bowl right back into Thomas's.

"Very well, Pietro Orsini, kneel on the floor for the rest of the meal," he ordered.

Pietro climbed over the bench and knelt down. For a moment he sat back on his heels, but Dom Cuthbert seized him by the shoulder and forced him to kneel erect.

"That," Dom Cuthbert informed Thomas, "is what happens to boys who do not behave like gentlemen here. Pietro will have nothing to eat until breakfast." Thomas was too stunned to reply, but he felt very grateful to Dom Cuthbert for rescuing his supper.

After supper (or collation, as it is called in the monastery), the boys played again until compline, the night prayer of the Church. Thomas stood on the sidelines by himself, for Dom Cuthbert had left him to have his own supper. Then Pietro and Giovanni came up to him and looked him over, up and down. They were both a couple of years older than Thomas, but they were not much taller, for Thomas took after his tall Norman ancestors. And they were dark-haired, dark-skinned, and quick with the tongue. For some reason, Thomas felt he wasn't going to enjoy the encounter one bit.

Pietro spoke first. "So you're Thomas Aquinas, the lord abbot's spy," he said, a threatening smile on his lips, as though he hadn't forgotten about the episode at the supper table.

Thomas was startled, but he was an Aquino, and, as his father always said, an Aquino always defends himself, even if he is only five—and pretty scared. "I am Thomas Aquinas, but I am not the lord abbot's spy. He is my Granduncle Sinebald," he protested hotly.

"We know," said Giovanni. "We saw you talking to him. And your father, too. You'll be running to tell him everything—"

"Yes, and the only reason you're here is because—because of what your father did to the abbey. We know about you, and your cousin Emperor Frederick, who would murder the pope himself if—"

Thomas looked from one to the other. This was all news to him. All the pride of the Aquinos rose up in him, but he was so shocked that he couldn't say anything better than "That's a lie!"

"Oh, is it? You'll find out!" said Pietro. And the two boys, sensing trouble, scampered away. Dom Cuthbert was on the scene again. There were tears in Thomas's eyes.

"Tears, Thomas!" He took the small boy's hand and led him to a cool stone bench along the courtyard wall, and sat down. Still holding his hand, he looked tenderly and intently at the boy, and said, "Now, Thomas, you tell me all about it."

"Pietro and Giovanni said—that—my father did something bad to the monastery and that he put me here to pay back. Father Cuthbert, what did he do? And my cousin Emperor Frederick, is he bad to the pope?"

Dom Cuthbert put his head back against the wall. "Oh, so that's it!" he said, laughing gently. "Well, Thomas, just you forget about it. Those boys will be punished. They didn't show much charity, did they?"

"Please, Father, I don't know what that word is—char-i-ty."

"Charity is simply love of God and our neighbor, Thomas. When you love God you have to be kind to all God's people, too."

God? There it was again! Thomas was so much interested in this new idea about God that he almost forgot his trouble, but only for a moment. "But is it true—what they said, Father?"

"I suppose it is, Thomas, but it all happened before you were born—eleven years ago, in fact—and you are not to blame for it. There's nothing for you to do but be a good boy."

"But what did he do? My father, I mean," Thomas persisted.

"Well, lad, you may as well know. Your cousin the emperor is an enemy of Our Holy Father, and your father is one of the emperor's knights. Your father led the emperor's soldiers when they attacked Monte Cassino last time. But Thomas, you had nothing to do with it. Understand?"

Thomas was indignant and humiliated together. "But, Father, didn't the monks fight right back?"

"Fight back, Thomas? No, Benedictines never fight. Remember this afternoon when I showed you that big shield on the chapel floor—and what it said on it? *Pax*—Peace. We are here to make peace, not war."

"But couldn't you maybe *talk* to them so they would go over to our Holy Father's side?"

"Talk? No, we don't do any preaching either. We are silent men, Thomas. We speak only to God—through our prayer and work. Oh, we've been attacked many times, and we'll probably be attacked again—though God forbid! But I think we'd better get started for compline now," he said. He patted the worried head of the little boy and got to his feet.

Just then another big bell rang out, and the pair hurried toward the chapel. Again they waited against the wall while the monks and students filed in. There so many monks, and Thomas was sure he could never learn to tell them apart, except for Dom Cuthbert, of course. Besides, all the other monks had black cowls over their heads tonight, so that you couldn't see even the tips of their noses. For all Thomas knew, they might have been the very same monks who had come to Monte Cassino with St. Benedict when he built the first Monte Cassino seven hundred years ago. Thomas had never heard of St. Benedict before that afternoon, but he decided he must have been pretty wonderful if all these monks still did just what he had told his first monks to do if they were going to serve God and become saints. Like his tall friend Dom Cuthbert here....

The boys were something else again. Just now Thomas felt that they were all his enemies. They probably all knew about his family's wickedness and would never have anything to do with him. Here he was: the son of Count Landolph of Aquino and Lord of Belcastro and Loretto, a distant cousin of the new king of France, a godson of Pope Honorius III, and nephew of the lord abbot himself. Up to now he had been proud of it. But here at Monte Cassino it was a disgrace to be an Aquino—although they might possibly forgive you for being an Aquino.

This was a pretty stiff lesson for Thomas's first day at school, and it would take him many years to learn it—maybe (who knows?) the rest of his life. All he knew now was that his little world of Roccasecca had tumbled down. He was embarrassed. Never again would he boast about his family or his cousins, even if people would henceforth think of him as a nobody.

Thomas felt the strong but gentle hand of Dom Cuthbert on his shoulder—the signal to move again. Dom Cuthbert led him to a chair at the end of the last row, so that, even if the smallest pupil was at the back of the huge chapel, he could see what was going on in front if he stuck his head out far enough. The monk reminded Thomas to genuflect (after all, Thomas hadn't had much experience with this sort of thing), then stood behind the boys, while the other monks seated themselves in the rows of choir stalls on both sides of the sanctuary to wait for the lord abbot to begin chanting the Divine Office. Thomas could barely see the little door where God was; in fact, God seemed far away in general just now.

Then the lord abbot ("my uncle," Thomas was just about to say to himself in a wave of family pride, when he suddenly remembered) arose and blessed himself, and all the monks and boys rose with him. The abbot sang out some words in Latin, and the monks answered him all together, and compline began. Thomas was all eyes and ears. He could not follow what they were saying, because it was in Church Latin, and at home and even at the abbey, people had got into the habit of using the language of the common people, called "Italian." But what he saw and heard enthralled him so much that he forgot about Giovanni and Pietro and how much he wished he were back at Roccasecca. It was all so beautiful and mysterious: the failing sunlight piercing through the windows above the high altar, the rows of black-hooded monks, their waving, reverberating chanting, the—well—holy atmosphere of everything, so different from what Thomas had known before. Thomas shivered a little. What did it all mean? It had something to do with God, he knew.

Then it was all over, and Dom Cuthbert appeared again to take him to the dormitory where he was to sleep with a number of the smaller boys. He noticed sleepily that Pietro had the cot next to his, but now he hardly cared. Even when he discovered that his cot was considerably less soft than his junior-sized manorial bed with the high canopy at home, he did not mind. He was interested only in falling asleep—which he promptly did.

I Want to Work for Truth

Thomas wandered to the playing field where the boys were beginning a game of mock-jousting—the first of the new fall term. It was just like the practice sessions he had watched in the bailey at Roccasecca, except that the boys did not have lances or horses like his big brothers; instead, they used sticks for weapons, and the bigger, heavier boys carried the lighter lads on their backs. Each pair would rush at the other, to try to knock the rider off his "horse's" back.

"Hey, Thomas," Pietro shouted as he saw Thomas emerge. "Come on, I'll mount you."

"All right," Thomas agreed, without too much interest. Thomas was no longer the "new boy," and the older boys had turned out to be not so much older—or smarter—than they had seemed that first day of school so long ago. And he knew that he was always welcome in this game because he was one of the tallest and strongest boys in the school. In fact, there was no boy in the school who could lift Thomas on his back.

With Pietro on his back, Thomas grasped his legs within his arms. Pietro kept his balance by putting his left hand around Thomas's neck. With his right hand, Pietro began to swing his stick, while Thomas lunged forward against their first opponents. They easily downed them. They continued to knock over every pair they met on the field. Thomas's body was so powerful, his grip so tight, his strategy so well thought out, that he could never be knocked off his feet.

"Thomas won again! Hooray for Thomas!" shouted Giovanni, one of the losers, when the game was over.

"No, it was Pietro," Thomas called back when he had caught his breath. Pietro slid off his "mount," and the two boys sauntered to the sidelines where their third buddy was sitting. It was dusk now, and nearly time for compline, and after that they would have another hour of study before bed.

"Look, Thomas," said Pietro, "why do you always give everybody else credit for what you do? You know perfectly well that I couldn't have done a thing if it hadn't been for you. You'll never get ahead in the world that way." They sat down on the bench beside their comrade Giovanni.

"How do you know, Pietro?" countered Giovanni from the other side of Thomas. "Maybe he'll get ahead of us all—with all the learning in that big skull of his. Say, by the way, Thomas, do you understand that new theorem in geometry? Hey, Thomas, wake up!"

Thomas wasn't asleep, but he had something else on his mind. "Yes, I understand it, Giovanni. All you have to remember is—but let's wait till we get to the study hall so that we can work it out together on paper—if Dom Cuthbert gives us permission to talk."

"Good old Thomas. Knew you'd come through." Giovanni put his arm around his friend. Although both Giovanni and Pietro were fifteen years old, Thomas, who was only thirteen, had soon caught up with them in school. They respected him as much for his mind as for his physical power and his generosity in helping them out. He got his lessons so well that he made them gasp at times.

"Hey, Thomas," said Pietro abruptly. "Heard from my father today. It's all set for Salerno. I'm accepted for the medical school—best in the world. No wars for me—I've got enough brothers to carry on the Orsini family honor."

Thomas smiled happily at Pietro. "That's great, Pete. Healing people is much better than killing them, isn't it? And with you studying law at Bologna"—Thomas looked toward Giovanni on his left—"the Caetani family—"

"The Caetani family? No, what I'm going to do is try to get some justice for the serfs and peasants, just the way you were telling me that time. But what about you, Thomas? Suppose you'll have to go to the University of Naples?"

"I—I don't know. . .But what makes you think that?"

"Because your Holy Roman Emperor cousin"—Giovanni bowed his head in mock homage—"has decreed that if you live anywhere near Naples you can't go anywhere but to his shiny new university."

"It's not so bad, Johnny," interrupted Pietro. "Father and I looked it over this summer. Emperor Frederick's got the right idea. He's brought in all sorts of famous scholars and teachers and pays their expenses and helps out the students, too, and he's let in some new kind of begging preachers who really know the answers. After all, Frederick's quite a mind himself, even if he is excommunicated. Thomas could suffer a worse fate than to have to go to Naples. Might've gone there myself if—hey, Thomas!" Thomas was lost in thought again. "Here we've got your future all settled and—"

Thomas locked his hands between his knees and said, "I wish my future were that simple to settle." He seemed quite miserable.

Giovanni took his arm away from Thomas's shoulder, and whispered sympathetically, "Something go wrong at home, Thomas?"

Thomas nodded his head but did not speak, and all three were suddenly silent. It was then that they noticed that Dom Cuthbert had come from somewhere and was standing soundlessly beside the three friends. His fringe of hair ("tonsure," the monks called it) had grayed during the last eight years, but his eyes were still cool blue (he was English, they had learned long ago), and he hadn't lost his mysterious way of appearing where he hadn't been a second before. The boys jumped to their feet.

"Could an old monk join you young gentlemen for a moment before compline?" Giovanni and Pietro shot a look at each other, then Pietro said, "Oh sure, Dom Cuthbert. You stay and console Brother Thomas. Come, Giovanni, we can hit the books for a bit before compline."

When the two had departed, Dom Cuthbert sat down with Thomas. "What's this about consoling you, Thomas? Everything all right at home?"

Thomas looked up to meet the penetrating look of his teacher. "No, Father," he said. "Everything's about as all wrong as possible."

"Oh, come now—is it as bad as all that?"

"It's—well, they just don't look at things the way I do."

Dom Cuthbert smiled. "To impatient young men about to begin their work in the world, parents always seem behind the times. Later on, we sometimes find that our parents were right and we were wrong."

"But they don't even begin to see my problem. Ever since Father Abbot Sinebald died they keep writing about my taking his place. They've given up trying to make a soldier out of me, but if I'm to be a monk, it's got to be as the lord abbot of Monte Cassino or nothing! And Father, I couldn't go into the Benedictines knowing that my parents were going to use pressure to make me lord abbot."

"Well, you are a bit young for a job like that." Again Dom Cuthbert smiled. "But maybe in time—"

Thomas faced his old teacher. "Dom Cuthbert, I don't think I even want to be a monk. I want to go on searching for God. I love Monte Cassino more than anything in the world, but—" Thomas frowned and bit his lip.

"Go on, Thomas. Perhaps if you asked yourself, what is it you really want to do with your life?"

"That's just what my family wanted to know, and I couldn't give them an answer. But I think I want to work for truth—fight for it, die for it. You once told me what St. Benedict said to his monks: 'Seek peace and follow it.' And I've remembered it all these years. But, Father, it looks to me as though seeking peace is just not enough nowadays, when people like Emperor Frederick are trying to destroy our religion, and the poor people don't know what to believe anymore. Oh, Father, I'm so sorry, after all the Benedictines have done for me—"

"Dear boy, we're friends, aren't we?—very old friends. We can certainly be honest with each other. Now listen: the monks here have done no more for you than for any other boy who came here to be educated. It there was ever a student of whom we could be proud, it's you, Thomas. And we'd be mighty sorry to lose you. But look, Thomas—uh-oh, there goes the bell—you have a whole school year in front of you. Don't try to force a decision tonight. It will come with grace and prayer. All right?"

The two old friends moved toward the chapel, as they had done every night for almost ten years.

Flight

The decision came suddenly and violently, and not the way Dom Cuthbert or Thomas Aquinas had imagined it. It came on a summer morning, not long before Thomas and his friends were to finish their secondary course at Monte Cassino. And it came with an armed rider from Roccasecca who demanded Thomas at once. The lay brother who admitted him went running to find the headmaster, Dom Cuthbert, and Dom Cuthbert found Thomas in the study hall at his logic exercises. Thomas scrambled out of his desk and his thoughts to face his teacher.

"Well, Thomas, this is it," said Dom Cuthbert grimly. "Get your things—and fast. You're going home—immediately!"

"But why?"

"Not a word, Thomas!" Dom Cuthbert was fierce now. "Here, I'll go with you."

Together they clipped up to the senior dormitory, found Thomas's saddlebags, stuffed his books and a few pieces of clothing into them, raced down again and out to the waiting horseman. Then Dom Cuthbert spoke: "You may never see Monte Cassino again, Thomas. Kneel down quickly, and let me give you my—my last—blessing."

Thomas stood dumbfounded.

"Thomas, kneel! I must get back to the other boys!"

Thomas knelt on the pavement. The Aquino courier took off his cap, bowed his head. Dom Cuthbert made the blessing and laid his two hands on Thomas's head. Then he gently touched the boy's elbow, bidding him to rise. He took the boy's hands and pressed them to his heart, then turned and went into the building without a word.

As soon as they were outside the abbey gates, the horseman leaned over from his mount and said, "Thomas, I disobeyed my lord your father. I will be killed if he ever finds out. I told the monk what was going to happen—so they could escape and save their lives." He crossed himself.

"What—what are you talking about, Philippo? Where are we going?"

"Look down yonder, Thomas."

The morning mists were just rising out of the valley. In their place rose the smoke of a hundred burning cottages and barns and cowsheds. When Thomas looked closer he saw a forest of pointed spears, then the warriors themselves, mounted, and dressed in full armor. Thomas closed his eyes in utter misery.

"Thomas, you won't tell your lord father?"

"Tell my father what?—oh, of course not. You did the right thing to warn the monks. These are the enemies of God. Come, Philippo, we must hurry. We've got to get to the emperor." Thomas spurred ahead down the rock-strewn trail.

Philippo caught up with him, reached out for Thomas's bridle. "No, Thomas, it's no use. They're only waiting till you get past before they attack. They need the abbey's position to fight the pope's army . . . But now the monks may have time to escape—because I warned them."

"But the emperor may listen to me. We can't let this happen, Philippo!"

"You—a chit of a boy? When they've been planning this campaign for years? Not on your life!" The henchman took a new grip on Thomas's bridle, holding his own reins in the same hand. "Here's where we turn off. We're taking the roundabout way."

With his right hand he raised his lance high into the air in some sort of signal to the troops below, and then led Thomas's horse after his own down a narrow pass across the valley from the emperor's waiting army.

Chapter 3: Friars of Naples

Naples

"You know, Tom, I didn't like that bloody business any more than you did."

Thomas, turning in his saddle, looked sharply at Ronald, his next oldest brother. "Which bloody business?"

"Oh, you know—sacking Monte Cassino and all that."

"Oh." Thomas looked straight ahead again. All the bitter grief of the past summer welled up in the fifteen-year-old's heart. He was trying hard to forget, but something or somebody was always reminding him of it again. Monte Cassino, where he had lived for some ten happy years from 1230 to 1240, had been looted and burned, the farmers' homes and crops destroyed, and some of the monks, including his beloved Dom Cuthbert, murdered in cold blood. He closed his eyes to try to blot it out . . . But now he had to say something: Ronald was doing his best to make up for what had happened. "Anyway, you had nothing to do with it, Ronald."

They had been idling after a long climb, but now they picked up speed. Suddenly, as they rounded another promontory, the bay of Naples came into sight, and both boys halted their horses to catch the beauty of it: the ruffled deep blue water, the slanting ships with their sails puffed by the wind, reaching into port or bearing out to sea, the closely gathered, yellow-ochre-walled, red-roofed houses gleaming in the sun, the great dome of the blue September sky. All these things, Thomas mused, thought up by God and revealed to man through his own eyes and ears and adding up to something called Naples!

Ronald spoke first. "I'd chuck everything to be a poet at a time like this!"

Thomas sat back in his saddle. "You are already a poet, Ronnie."

"Who, me? No, Tom, 'fraid it's a little late for that . . . But let's get moving. I've got to see that you get to the university so that you can bring new glory upon your family." (Ronald was always teasing him a little bit.) "Poor old Thomas—what a trial you are! You talk the family out of making a soldier of you, and they insist you have to be lord abbot of Monte Cassino. When you talk them out of that, then you have to be the star of the university! Who knows, maybe the emperor will take notice of you and make you *rector magnifico*—the big boss. Guess I don't envy you so much after all!"

Ronald snapped his reins and got a new grip on his lance, and they set off cantering down a sloping trail that led into town. There was no chance for talk now, but Thomas was thinking how right Ronald was—he loved his family, but they were so ambitious, always trying to think of ways to please the emperor, never of pleasing God. If only they could understand that he wasn't interested in being successful or famous or powerful; you couldn't spend ten years with those humble, kindly Benedictines and still act as if this were the only world. Now, with Dom Cuthbert dead, Thomas felt as though there wasn't anyone to take his side. He felt like an orphan, for he didn't feel at home at Roccasecca anymore, and he had lost his abbey home. And, as is usual with fifteen year olds, he began to feel very sorry for himself—but not for long.

"Hey, Thomas, watch where you're going!" called Ronald sharply. They were approaching a thronged street corner in the heart of the city, and Thomas's horse had almost toppled an herb-vender's cart. The peddler was shaking his fist and gesticulating madly at the young nobles. Thomas jerked his reins and came alongside Ronald.

"Boy, that was a narrow escape. But I was looking at that odd monk who just went by." He turned in his saddle for another look. The "monk" had disappeared by now, but Thomas couldn't forget his peculiar outfit—a white habit with a black cappa, or cloak (his Benedictines wore just black), and a hood thrown back on his shoulders. He had a "tonsure" like the monks, on the top of his head. And he seemed to be in a great hurry.

"Well, you'll either kill yourself or somebody else if you start looking at those pesky friars. The town is thick with them."

"Friars?"

"Sure, that's what he is, a friar—a begging friar at that," said Ronald, unable to conceal his contempt. "The emperor has installed them at his university." Thomas was silent but thinking hard.

"Well, here we are, Tom." They were at the gates of the monastery where Thomas was going to live, at least till he got his bearings. The boys dismounted. "I won't go in with you. Your stuff will be down from Roccasecca tomorrow. I'll be back in town before you know it—and of course Mother will be coming to check up on your progress. Well, Thomas, have fun!"

The two boys hugged each other like a pair of bear cubs. Then Ronald mounted his horse and rode away, leading Thomas's horse behind him. Thomas rather forlornly turned in through the open gates of San Severino. The monks were expecting him, and they all welcomed him as one of their "old boys" from Monte Cassino. Thomas felt very grateful to them, but he couldn't get that "friar" out of his head.

Master Peter

"Well, Thomas of Aquin, do you know who Aristotle was?"

Master Peter of Ireland was striding up and down before his reading stand in a state of exasperation. First day of school, and already he was thinking of returning to Ireland. Every year the new students seemed more stupid than the last—shouldn't even be allowed inside a university; all they thought of was the good time they had had last night or were going to have tonight. He took his eyes from the roll of names in his left hand and looked down at the roomful of freshmen sitting on their straw mats—all that separated them from the cold, hard, stone floor. "Never encountered such a bunch of noodle-headed clowns before in all my years of teaching," he mumbled as he waited for Thomas of Aquin to identify himself from some part of the classroom.

Slowly from the back of the room a tall, sandy-haired, sun-browned youth got to his feet. Master Peter stood still and waited. "Well, Thomas of Aquin?"

"Please, Master Peter," Thomas answered almost apologetically, "Aristotle was a Greek philosopher who discovered truth three centuries before Christ."

This was almost too great a shock for Master Peter. He threw back his head, narrowed his flashing black eyes for another look at this young giant. Then he covered his surprise and decided to draw the boy out a bit.

"But I thought that was what Christ came on earth to do. Don't tell me this Aristotle had already taken care of all that—"

"No, Master Peter," Thomas answered, more calmly than he felt. "All Aristotle did was show that even a pagan can find the truth by using his own mind to reason with."

"That will do, Thomas of Aquin," Master Peter roared. "See me after class."

The other boys, hungry for something to laugh at, laughed at Thomas as he lowered himself to his mat again. Here was the ideal victim for them—this big, slow-moving, slow-speaking yokel. But their laughter was short-lived. Master Peter bellowed, "And that, gentlemen, is what you are going to do in my philosophy classes: use your own minds to reason with—or out you go!"

"Go on, Thomas." This was not the flashing-eyed old Irishman, but one of the begging friars —in fact, the very one who had caught Thomas's eye as he and Ronald were coming into Naples. He was dressed in white, and kept fingering the string of black beads looped from his leather belt. He was called John of San Juliano. The two of them were sitting in a tiny, unadorned parlor in their new monastery (only they called it a convent) next door to their church in the middle of town.

"Well, Father John, when all the boys had left, Master Peter said 'How did you happen to learn about Aristotle?' And I told him I had helped the monks at Monte Cassino to copy out his books; you know how the monks keep making copies to supply all their other monasteries." Father John nodded his understanding. "But I wasn't much good at it, because I am a very bad writer and, besides, I got so much interested in what I was copying that I just read ahead instead and tried to remember what I was reading. So they gave me another job."

Father John laughed in great amusement. "And what then?"

"Well, Master Peter said 'It's a pity you can't get into the theology school till you've finished your liberal arts course because that's where you belong.'"

Father John leaned forward in interest. "Why do you think he said that?"

"I—I don't know, Father—unless—" (Thomas brightened as an idea dawned on him) "—unless it's because I told him that all I wanted to study was about God—and that's what theology is." Thomas paused and then went on, "And maybe that's why he told me I ought to go and see the Dominican friars."

"Could be," mused Father John. "We are the theology faculty after all."

"But Father, it took me all this time to get up enough courage. I've been going to your church for weeks, and I've listened to your sermons, and I've followed the friars around the streets, and I know all about Dominic too, and how he took Truth for his motto and how he's changed everybody's minds about fighting our enemies—and I always felt that it was better to tell other people about the things of God than just to think about them—and how he made his men get educated so that they would know more about God—and all. And he made them be poor and stay poor so they wouldn't get ambitious. But it wasn't till Sunday, when you told the Gospel story about how the Apostles left everything to follow Christ, that I decided that I'd simply have to talk to you. I just sort of felt that this was what I was looking for all the time and didn't know it. And here I am."

"How old are you, Thomas?"

"Fifteen, Father," said Thomas, a little ashamed.

"A ripe old age, that," teased Father John. "Three or four more years as a liberal arts student is going to make a big difference."

"Oh no, Father!" Thomas contradicted. "It isn't like that—I'm not going to change. Please take me right now!"

"'Take you,' Thomas?"

"Yes, Father. I want to be a Dominican. I want to start right now."

"Now look, Thomas, let's be reasonable. Five years ago we accepted a young noble like you and his folks stoned our priory and almost murdered us—that despite the fact that our Father Dominic had a few royal relations himself! Secondly, you are three years too young. Our constitutions wouldn't allow us to take you till you are eighteen. Until then, you owe your obedience to your parents and your teachers. But, Thomas, that doesn't mean we can't be good friends. You will always be welcome here. We will be praying that you find God's will—and do it. That's a promise!" Father John rose as if to end the discussion.

"Oh, Father John—" Thomas was so full of emotion that he didn't know what to say.

"Now here, Thomas, I want you to have this rosary. It's just a smaller version of the one I have on my belt. I'll show you how to use it. This is our favorite Dominican prayer, because Our Lady herself recommended it to Father Dominic. I'm sure that Our Lady and Dominic between them will see you through."

Dominicans

After that interview, Thomas's life took on new excitement. Of course life in a big university teeming with boys was exciting enough, but Thomas had other reasons. He had a secret, a very precious secret: he was going to be a Dominican. Nothing would stop him. He was going to prove to Father John that he had a real, sincere vocation to Father Dominic's Order of Preachers if it took forever—and four years looked like forever to him just now.

Meantime he concentrated for all he was worth on his classes. His classmates had long ago given up tempting him with their invitations to drinking and sporting. Like the boys at Monte Cassino, they first began to admire him for his mind and then to love him for himself, and some of them even tried to follow his good example. He was always so courteous and helpful to everybody that he won a whole army of friends without even knowing it. In fact, he tried not to draw any attention to himself. He would have been startled out of his wits if anyone had told him that the eyes of the whole campus were upon him, and that the Holy Roman Emperor Frederick was more than pleased at the record his young kinsman was making at his new university. Thomas had something more important on his mind, and in every free moment he was learning all he could about the Dominicans, and how he could best prepare to be one of them.

But he had not reckoned with his family. For three years he kept his secret from them because he was certain they would be upset, and he did not like to upset anyone, least of all his family. But now the time had come. It was on his last vacation at home before his last term in college. He was going on eighteen, and—if all went well—the Dominicans could soon admit him to their order.

His mother had planned a big feast that evening as a farewell for her youngest child, now so tall and grown-up. Count Landolph, looking gray and haggard and tired of a life of warfare, gave her her seat at the hostess's end of the long, overloaded table, and then took his place at the head. The four other children who were still at home—the pretty girls Marotta and Theodora, the war-hardened boys Ronald and Landolph Jr.—spaced themselves around their parents. Thomas sat in the middle, his heart in his mouth, unable to eat. Page boys trooped in and out with sumptuous roasts and pastries and fruits.

At last the business part of the banquet was finished, and Count Landolph cleared his throat for a little speech. "The emperor," he began, "is very proud of you, Thomas."

"And well he should be," Countess Theodora added, smiling happily on Thomas. Ronald shot a glance at Thomas, who was staring at his plate in confusion. Landolph Jr. took a big swallow of wine. The girls murmured their admiration.

"You know, Thomas," his father continued, "we want only the best for you. We were wrong to think that you could ever be happy as abbot of Monte Cassino, but now there is no doubt about your future. Mother and I have discussed it. The emperor is very much interested in his university, but so far it hasn't turned out enough real scholars to match Paris or Oxford. That's why he is delighted with your record. So, you are to continue your studies until he can see his way to make you *rector magnifico* of the university. How do you like that?" Count Landolph smiled, expecting a gasp of gratitude from his youngest son.

"Please, Father, I don't like it."

Count Landolph blustered, "You don't like the chance to be head of a university? And why not, pray tell? You like to study and you like books. What more can you want?"

"What I want is to be a Dominican friar—if they will have me."

There now: it was out at last. Thomas looked up and faced his father.

"A friar!" His father spat out the words. He seized his goblet and swallowed a gulp of wine.

"Are you mad, Thomas?" his mother shrieked.

"'—if they will have him,' he says." This from Landolph Jr. "Mighty choosy for a band of beggars, eh, Father?"

"Should have made a soldier out of him in the first place—like me," Ronald put in, mockingly, and almost under his breath. "Then we wouldn't have any problems." Nobody felt like enjoying his joke.

"My being a Dominican should be no problem to any of you," Thomas said quietly.

"Thomas," his father said, more calmly now, "are you really serious about joining the beggars—living off the alms of good people?"

Marotta didn't give Thomas a chance to answer. "They're just common riffraff, Thomas. Haven't you any pride?" she scolded.

"No more than I can help. Besides, Marotta, our holy—" (he was about to say "our holy founder" but quickly caught himself) "the founder Dominic was a noble and so is Albert of Cologne and lots of others in the order, only they don't go around bragging about it. And they're priests and brothers and they have degrees from the universities and—"

"But Thomas," pleaded the younger sister, Theodora, "you are just a boy. By the time you've finished at the university those Dominicans will be forgotten. They have no history or tradition or—why, they're no better than the Franciscans!" Theodora shuddered at the thought.

"And what's so wrong with the Franciscans?" Thomas shot back, remembering how Dominic and Francis had miraculously recognized each other in Rome, and then embraced each other in Christ-like love. "Give them time, Theo. Father Dominic died only twenty years ago, and already he is being made a saint."

Count Landolph had had enough of this. He rose to his feet, his face flushed with anger. "You'll be a Dominican friar over my dead body!" he roared, as he threw his massive baronial chair out of his way and stomped out of the banquet hall.

The banquet broke up in a hurry. Thomas had done it again.

Thomas was a pretty sad young man when he registered for the new term. When he told his trouble to Father John, the Dominican replied very casually, "What did you expect, Thomas? If everything went smoothly, you could be sure that something was wrong. And remember, Our Lord waited nearly thirty years before He began His public ministry. I daresay we'll all survive till you are free. Patience, Thomas, patience!"

Count Landolph was killed later that month in September 1240—pierced with a lance and thrown from his mount on the emperor's new campaign against the pope. Thomas was crushed with the horror of it. His father's parting words, "Over my dead body," kept ringing in his mind—as though Thomas had had something to do with his death! At first he was so shocked that it didn't even occur to him that now he was really free. All he could think of was to pray for his father—and his mother, too. Sometimes he wept when he was praying. The months and years passed on.

One evening, when he was kneeling before the tabernacle of the priory church, he felt a light tap on his shoulder. He turned around to see Father John standing beside him, all kindness and compassion. Thomas was ashamed of his reddened eyes and the tears that stood there waiting to fall. "Thomas, come, it is time. You have waited—and suffered—long enough."

Brother Thomas

Thomas's reception into the order was a quiet little ceremony in the priory chapel. Father John feared that the Aquinas family might make trouble if they knew. But all the friars—priest, student brothers, and lay brothers— were there; so, even if Thomas had just lost his father (and probably his family besides), he had just acquired hundreds of spiritual fathers and brothers. And they all chanted the beautiful Pentecost hymn *Veni, Creator Spiritus* as Father Ambrose, the novice master, and one of the lay brothers helped Thomas into his new white habit.

Then, when Thomas looked every inch a Dominican, even to the rosary hanging from his belt, Father John gave him a stern little sermon, rather like a commander to his soldiers before the big battle. The whole community broke into a happy *Te Deum* (the great hymn of praise) and the ceremony was over. And then, the "kiss of peace"—when every single Dominican, from the master general down, gave their brand-new brother a hearty embrace, some of the young ones adding a smack to his ribs to show how glad they were.

Thomas felt that he was really home for the first time. And he was hoping he would never have to leave home again.

Figure 2   Thomas becoming a Dominican

Chapter 4: Castle Captive

To Rome

As soon as the friars had cleared the chapel, Father John seized his new novice by the sleeve. "Now, Brother Thomas, everything is ready," he said. "You leave for Rome immediately. The master general will accompany you."

"You mean—I can't stay here?"

"No questions, Brother." Father John sternly put his finger to his lip, and Thomas mastered the lesson of instant obedience in a hurry.

It was not until they were well out of Naples on the road to Rome that the two friars paused long enough to get their breath.

"Whee! Only a hundred and fifty miles to go!" said Father John the Teuton, Master General of the Dominicans, as he threw himself on the grass and stuck a long blade in his mouth. "Bet you never walked that much before in your life." Father John patted the grass beside him as an invitation for Thomas to sit down. "Relax, Thomas. If your family comes after you, they'll have to go to Naples first, and we're going the other way."

Thomas sat down beside his companion and stretched out his long legs. "What I can't see," he said, continuing the talk they were having earlier, "is how the Dominicans figure they will be any safer with me out of Naples. My mother could ruin our order no matter where I am. I didn't realize how much trouble I could cause."

"Forget it, Brother. All in a day's work. And nothing's going to happen to our order on account of you. When you've seen as much blood and thunder as I have—but let's get going. There's a Cistercian abbey we can head to for the night, not much farther on. Poor Brother Thomas—spending his first night as a Dominican in a Cistercian monastery."

They were striding along with Father John setting the pace. It took them a week to get to Rome, skirting the highways, begging for food, hunting up monasteries for the night, watching for kidnappers in ambush, singing their lovely Dominican hymns and taking turns at the Divine Office when the footing was smooth enough. Finally the old capital city of Rome spread itself out before them. Thomas wanted to linger to take in the view, but Father John hustled him right on until they had climbed the Aventine Hill to Santa Sabina, an ancient basilica that the pope had given to Dominic for his headquarters.

The travelers were hardly inside the gates of Santa Sabina when Thomas was dispatched on his way again. A courier from Naples taking the fast highway had beaten the friars to Rome, with the news that Thomas's mother had already been to Naples and had threatened to have the emperor's army seize Thomas by force if the friars refused to give him up. And Thomas's very own brothers were camping with the emperor's forces at Aqua Pendente, waiting for a signal to besiege Santa Sabina itself.

"They have a warrant from the emperor to arrest you, Brother Thomas," explained the prior. "You haven't a moment to lose. So—on to Bologna with the master general and a couple of brand-new friars. There you will be beyond the power of your cousin the emperor before you go on to Paris."

"But I have a relative in Paris, Father Prior. He's Louis IX—oh, I'm sorry, I shouldn't have said that."

"Why not? King Louis is a very good friend of the friars, and I don't think he will interfere with your vocation." Then, addressing the travelers, he added, "Now, here is some food for the trip, and God be with you." The prior gave his blessing to the young friars, while a lay brother put a bundle of bread and cheese and fruit into their knapsack. "And remember—keep off the highways!"

Toward Bologna

They had been walking and talking all night—all of two nights, in fact—or, more correctly, Father John did the talking and his three young friars took it all in. Father John had taught so long at the university that he felt like a native son of Bologna despite his German identity. It was his "very special city, the dearest inheritance of his heart," as it had been for Jordan of Saxony, whom Dominic himself had chosen as his successor to head the order. As master general of the order, Father John had convoked a general chapter for this year 1244 and had invited Thomas and the other brothers along on their way to Paris. He figured that there was no better way to initiate the novice Dominicans into the life of their Holy Founder and the spirit of the order than to let them observe a general chapter in operation—in addition to the need to give Thomas's family the slip. And he said as much as they trudged along toward Bologna.

"But why," put in Brother Robert, "do we have to watch what happens at a general chapter when we already know beforehand how it is going to turn out? Like that first one on Pentecost."

"Like that one—indeed," Father John repeated, turning on his defenseless challenger. "Don't you think you would have learned anything from seeing the representatives of the whole order coming together and struggling over the big job of working out the Constitutions and Rule so that they would last not just for now but for the future?"

"Well, how about the second chapter?"

"As for the second one, when they carved out the five territories we call provinces—Spain, France, Provence, Lombardy, and Rome —Father Dominic appointed a superior (provincial) for each. But by then he was a worn-out, dying man. Next question?"

Brother Timothy spoke up. "Didn't the monks—er, friars—" Father John raised a shocked eyebrow at the offending word—"try to take care of their founder and make him well again?"

"They did everything they could, Brother. They even carried him way up the hill to Santa Maria del Monte, where it was cool and breezy, when the summer heat in Bologna down below was enough to kill a much younger man. But when Dominic realized he was going to die, he asked to be carried back to San Nicolas."

"Then why didn't they put Dominic on a donkey and let him ride back? Even Our Lord—"

"Because," Father John replied, "we are trying to live like the very first Christians, who were living their poverty as in the Gospels. So we aren't allowed to use animals for transportation. "Is that why we really have no place to call our home, and why we have to go begging?"

"Yes," Father John agreed. "And we can skip chanting the Psalms if we have to study instead, and why we live in the middle of the big cities when we might prefer to enjoy the country."

"But, Father," chimed in Brother Robert, "why couldn't they have just joined up with the Franciscans and saved a lot of wear and tear? Dominic and Francis were buddies, weren't they?"

"Up to a point, Brother. You see, from the start ours was an order of priests—and Francis was never a priest. And there was nothing romantic about our rule of life. It was all geared to winning souls, so that our preaching has to be just as intellectual as it is spiritual; and as soon as new friars might begin to feel at home in their study house, off they must go to the best universities—like Bologna."

"But if our order is on the right track, how come it's taken so long to make Father Dominic a saint when Francis got there in two years?"

"Because we've been too busy, that's why," snapped Father John. "Making saints is way down on our list of priorities. Just to think what a job it was to reorganize those Roman nuns so they could move into Saint Agnes's convent in Bologna—"

So far Thomas had been quietly thinking his own thoughts, being sorry they had had to leave Santa Sabina so fast (though he had a feeling he'd be returning soon), and glad for the detour to Bologna (St. Dominic's tomb was there). But at the mention of Saint Agnes, one of his favorite saints, Thomas was all ears.

"First," the master general related, "Dominic had to collect the nuns from across the Tiber and settle them at Saint Sixtus (his first base in Rome) together with a couple of nuns from Prouille (converts from the Albigensians) and prepare them to take over the convent going up at Bologna. Two of the refugees from their run-down convent really got the Bologna convent on its feet, and one of them, Sister Cecilia, the first prioress, lived sixty more years and well into her nineties, and could remember every detail about Father Dominic.

"But," continued Father John, "the very first impetus to plant a convent of nuns at Bologna came from Diana, a local girl, a bouncy, feisty, spoiled daughter of the powerful d'Andolo clan, who fell in love with the new order when she heard a sermon by Dominic's companion Reginald of Orléans. She got Dominic's permission for a convent of young women like herself—just before he took off for a meeting in Venice and returned to Bologna a dying man."

"Was that when Saint Agnes's got going?" asked Thomas.

"Not quite yet," Father John replied. "Diana's family had convulsions when they caught wind of her intention. She went into hiding with some Augustinian nuns, but her brothers found her and dragged her home after a scuffle that cost her several broken ribs. Still imprisoned when Dominic died, she escaped again to the Augustinians while waiting for Saint Agnes's to be finished. By then she had a new protector, Master General Jordan of Saxony, who gave Diana and the other women the Dominican habit in 1223."

"Did Diana live a long time like Cecilia?"

"No, only a dozen more years," he answered with a sigh. Then brightening he added, "But she left a legacy of priceless letters from Jordan, her counselor and confidant."

No doubt Thomas was carried away by the story of this girl, and how hideously cruel it was of her brothers to try to prevent her from doing the will of God, just like his own family. But now, thank God, his worries were over—he was free at last.

Apprehended

The little troupe was investigating the last of the Santa Sabina provisions before knocking off for some sleep. They motioned for Thomas to dig in, but he was lost in remembrance of his struggle—so like Diana's. "Come on, Brother Thomas, have something before we polish off everything," urged one of his mates. "Or do you believe in mortification even on the road? Remember, after this we start begging for our food."

"You've got me wrong," Thomas asserted. "I haven't the slightest problem about enjoying food, so long as we don't break God's commandments to obtain it. Mortification really has no value on its own. Why shouldn't God's friends enjoy the good food He gives us? And not only food, but also the other beautiful things—the world of nature and the work of artists, all creation—"

"What an optimist you are! . . . But Thomas," Father John suggested, "wouldn't that be centering our spiritual life on creation, not on the Creator?"

"Oh never, Father! Our creaturely perfection—" He left the sentence unfinished because suddenly a light flashed and jumped some hundred yards before them. They protectively pulled Thomas into the bushes. Another light appeared. And another. Then they knew what it was—flaming torches, carried by horsemen. They heard the clatter of horses pounding along the field the friars had been skirting.

"It's all up now," said Father John. "It's the emperor's men."

"Maybe they're not after us at all," whispered Thomas. "Let's duck into the woods."

"Too late. We're surrounded." Horsemen were coming at them from both sides now. "Look, Brother Thomas, don't offer any resistance, see? But they won't get by with this for very long. We have the pope on our side!" exclaimed Father John.

The emperor's troops brought their horses to a halt from both sides, and the two leaders lowered their torches to light up the black-cloaked friars. The first leader leaned back in his saddle and laughed triumphantly. "Well, well, at last we have caught up with the runaway friar!" It was a laugh and a voice that Thomas recognized at once—Landolph, his own brother. "And who are these gentlemen?"

"I am the master general of the Order of Preachers," answered Father John. "We are on our way to a meeting of our order."

"We have no warrant for *your* arrest, sir—or for these two young fellows—and no room for you in Thomas's dungeon. So, make yourselves scarce, gentlemen, and no word of this to anyone, unless you want a lance run through you. Men, let these friars through the ranks. And, Ronald, bring up the extra nag for our brother here."

"This is the silliest expedition I was ever in on," grumbled Ronald as he jumped off his mount and took the reins of another horse that a soldier had brought up from the rear. "What a nuisance you are, Thomas!" He held the horse by the bridle. "Well," he sighed, "climb on—we've got to make tracks!" He flung the reins at Thomas.

All of Thomas's fighting blood surged up now. But as he looked from one brother to the other, and behind them to the picked guard armed to the hilt, he realized that resistance was hopeless. He didn't want to get killed before being ordained a Dominican priest and doing something useful for the Church. He looked beyond the ranks to see if he could see his Dominican companions. There was Father John, tall against the thicket, vigorously nodding his head to tell Thomas to obey the orders. Then he held up his hand in a good-bye gesture.

"All right, men," Landolph bawled. "Return to camp. You will not be required for this expedition." The troops—all except a small group of guards—spurred off toward Aqua Pendente. The three Aquino brothers, with Thomas between his captors, and their henchmen before and behind them (just in case Thomas might attempt a getaway), began their long trip to Roccasecca.

Figure 3   Thomas: family captive: angelic chord

The Tower

After three days—which seemed an eternity for Thomas—they arrived at the castle. The gatekeepers had watched their approach from far down the valley. The household was alerted. Great flares were set at the drawbridge to light up their entry.

As they galloped over the drawbridge and clattered across the outer bailey, Thomas's heart began to sink, and his hopes with it. The castle was practically impregnable: if you were outside you couldn't get in unless you were welcome; once you were inside there was no way of escaping—unless they let you. What chance did he have now? He hadn't quite believed what Landolph had said about a dungeon, and he had even taught Ronald to say the rosary with him during those long stretches in the saddle; in fact, neither of his brothers seemed to have his heart in what he was doing. But now everything seemed as serious as could be.

When they drew up to the inner court, the two big brothers dismounted. Thomas hesitated, both because he was stiff after the non-stop round trip to and from Rome, and also because it occurred to him that perhaps now was the moment to escape. No—not a chance. When he stepped down he began to reel a bit. Landolph and Ronald immediately pinned his arms and marched him into the great hall of the castle.

Countess Theodora rose like a queen from her baronial chair, and came toward her sons. Marotto and Theodora were beside her. Thomas could only stand there, amazed at the change in his beautiful mother since his father's death. Suddenly, he felt conscience-stricken to have added to her sorrows.

"Behold, Mother, the runaway abbot, caught without a struggle," Landolph announced as he released his hold on Thomas.

"Quiet, Landolph," hissed Ronald. "This is no time for your jokes."

"Thomas, why have you done this to me?" cried his mother.

Thomas dropped on one knee and seized her hand and kissed it. "Mother, I did only what I had to do."

"What you had to do," she echoed. "Did you have to break my heart? Did you have to join those beggars and make a laughingstock of all of us? Did you have to—" She wrenched her hand away from her son's clasp.

Thomas interrupted quietly, "I did what was the will of God for me."

"The will of God!" Countess Theodora looked away, put her hand to her forehead as if she couldn't bear the sight of her son, and said, "Landolph, take him to the tower. I don't want to look at him. His supper will be brought to him. He will stay there until he changes his mind. Do you understand, Thomas?" The two girls shivered in pity.

"Perfectly, Mother."

The San Giovanni tower in the castle was a big round room with thick stone walls and a mammoth fireplace, and slits of arched windows too high up in the walls to permit a view of the country and too narrow to escape from—even if there had been a ladder on the other side, which there wasn't. But they were ideal for defending the castle. You could throw a lot of spears, or pour a lot of hot oil from them without running any risk yourself. A cot, table, and chair had been provided for the new prisoner, but otherwise the room was bare as could be.

A huge armed sentry stationed outside the heavy oak door drew himself to attention as Landolph marched his brother inside. Landolph returned half a minute later. Thomas heard him close the door, turn the heavy, squeaking lock, and hand the foot-long key to the sentry. "You are never to leave this door unguarded, understand?" Landolf said menacingly.

The powerful sentry responded, "Aye, aye, sir," with his left hand on the evil-looking dagger hanging from his belt.

Sisters

The seasons passed, winter into summer. Thomas was alone, cut off from the world.

The lock turned, the door creaked open. His sister Theodora took the tray from a page boy, and called in, "Here I come, Thomas."

Usually Theodora left the tray on the table, kissed her brother lightly on the forehead, and left. She was forbidden to speak to him, and he never tried to take advantage of her by asking questions or begging favors from her (though she and Marotta had secretly pooled their supply of quills and parchment to give him writing materials). Today she hovered over the table as Thomas shoved aside his writing and rose to greet her—for Thomas never forgot his manners even if he was in prison.

"Thank you again, Theo. I was getting hungry all right."

"Oh, don't thank me, Thomas. Every time I come up here I feel better for it. But—Thomas, do you realize what day this is?"

"Why, no, Theo. Without a missal or calendar of the saints I've lost all track."

"Well, it's the 365th day since you were put here. That's one thousand and ninety-five times that Marotta and I have come up with your meals between us, and you haven't changed the least bit all that time. In fact, you seem to get happier all the time. And never a word of complaint. I—I just don't see how you can stand it—here all alone and all." Theodora threw herself on the foot of Thomas's cot and cupped her chin in her hands.

"But I'm not alone, Theo. God is right here with me. As we Dominicans say, the world is our cloister. This is my cloister. But—" and his face saddened, "I do mind being away from my order."

"That's what we guessed—Marotta and I—and we've decided to do something about it!"

Thomas put down the piece of bread he had just broken off his loaf and turned grateful eyes toward his sister. "That's so kind of you, Theo. But what could you do? You don't want to get into trouble too."

"Here's what. Thomas, I—I'm going to be married. To the Count of Marisco." Theodora began to blush. Thomas was so surprised that he could only stare. "Oh, it's all right with Mother if that's what you're thinking. Guess she is so glad I'm not going to be a spinster forever. I'm twenty-four, Thomas—and that's old."

Thomas looked at his big sister. With her bright face and dark shining eyes, and playing with her long black braids, she didn't look at all like a spinster to him. "That's very good news, Theo," he said.

"Point is that Anthony—that's his name—knows all about you, and he doesn't like the situation any more than I do. He wants to help. So, if there is anything he can do for you or bring you from Naples—"

"Oh, do you think he could, well, see Father John of San Juliano and get me some books maybe?" Thomas was growing more excited. "Like the Holy Bible, and the Dominican Rule and Peter Lombard and Aristotle—and—" Thomas eyed his frayed white habit.

"—and a new habit—that's what you were going to say. And boy do you need it! I don't know how many times the Dominicans have been at the gates with a bundle for you, but they weren't allowed in. But I'm sure Anthony can smuggle things in. Even if Mother found out, she couldn't say anything to Anthony because—well, you may as well know—Emperor Frederick is losing every battle, and if the Hohenstaufens fall, the Aquinos fall right with them, and the Mariscos are mighty powerful in the north and might have to come to our rescue. So, it's quite simple. And before I forget it, Landolphand Ronald are home—and in a pretty black mood. So you may expect a visit—" Theodora jumped up as though just remembering that she wasn't supposed to talk to Thomas. She whispered in his ear, "I won't forget—about the books," and stole like a conspirator out of the room.

The Test

That was the longest visit Thomas had had for a full year. And that evening when Marotta brought in his supper, she lingered, too—at least long enough to whisper to him that she wanted to become a

Benedictine sister, just from his good example. Then she slipped out. He was surprised all over again, and even happier than he had been over Theodora's news. Maybe if he prayed hard enough his mother might change her attitude. And maybe even his brothers, he thought to himself.

Just then there was a tremendous racket outside the door. Thomas could hear Landolph shouting at the sentry, "Open it up, will you!" Ronald was saying, "Quiet, Landolph, take it easy." And the two warriors were in the tower. Thomas jumped to his feet to greet them. Then he saw that they had drunk too much wine to be polite.

"I see that friar's get-up hasn't rotted off you yet, Thomas!" said Landolph. "Perhaps I can help it along a bit." And he pulled a small dagger from his belt and gestured as though he would slit the habit from top to toe—and Thomas inside it. Thomas backed to the wall but said nothing. "Oh, you make it too easy for us," Landolph complained. "What sport is there in that?—won't even defend himself! Come on, Ronald—I have a better idea."

Landolph and Ronald never returned to the tower. But one night soon after their visit, when the girls and their mother were already in bed, Thomas had a new guest. This was a beautiful young woman dressed immodestly. She had slunk in without a sound and come up before him with a flashing smile as he sat thinking about God before the fireplace.

Thomas looked up in surprise, all kinds of thoughts and desires and attractions tempted him. He was confused. Then all the strength of the Aquinos rose up inside him. He seized a flaming log and flourished it wildly before the young woman. She shrieked and fled out of the room. Thomas heaved the door closed, and with the burning firebrand etched a great cross upon it. Then he tossed the brand back into the hearth, and, shaking from head to foot, he dropped to his knees before his cot. He prayed as he had never prayed before. "Please, God," he cried, "don't ever let me be tempted against purity again."

As he knelt there, he began to feel something stirring in the room, something like a soothing presence all around him. Just then he saw two smiling angel faces looking down on him. Without a word they dropped a knotted cord over his head and fastened it around his waist. Then they vanished from sight. That was God's answer to his prayer, God's promise to keep him pure in body and mind. Thomas threw himself on his bed and slept soundly and peacefully that night.

A Basket Case

The next morning the sentry handed Thomas a bundle: two new habits by special messenger from Father John of San Juliano, via the Count of Marisco. Thomas was overjoyed, for no young man ever treasured cleanliness and neatness more than he. Next thing he knew, Father John came himself to bring him books and encouragement and some lessons to study, and, most wonderful of all, the sacraments of Penance and Holy Communion. In fact, everything was suddenly so pleasant that Thomas was afraid it must be a dream—or maybe just a lull before some awful new punishment his family was thinking up.

But Father John assured him that it was no dream, or reprieve. In fact, he whispered, Thomas might be released any day now. The brand-new pope, Innocent IV, had just learned about Thomas's rough treatment and was furious that such a thing could happen to a member of a religious order—even if Thomas was the youngest member of the youngest of all religious orders, and even if his jailers were no less than the emperor's cousins. Pope Innocent wasn't afraid of the emperor: the papal army was beating the emperor's every day—which meant that soon, please God, the Church would be free of the state's control, free to give God's grace and save men's souls the way Christ intended it to. So Pope Innocent simply ordered Countess Theodora to give up her son or else the whole Aquino family would be excommunicated.

Meanwhile, Thomas went on studying his books, writing assignments for Father John (delivered by the Count of Marisco's men), helping Theodora and Marotta to get ready for their new vocations, and preparing for the days when Father John or one of the other friars could bring him Holy Communion (and that meant a three-day walk each way for them). He was very busy and he certainly wasn't sad.

Marotta danced playfully around him as she set down his tray. "Oh, Thomas, I'm going to miss this job. And to think I found my vocation carrying a tray!"

Thomas sensed that his sister was trying to be mysterious, but he asked innocently, "Are you leaving for the convent so soon, Marotta?"

"I'm not, but you are, Thomas."

"You mean—?"

Marotta nodded. "Just as soon as the Count of Marisco's weavers finish your basket."

"Marotta, you talk in riddles. What are you getting at?"

"It's all a big dark secret, and you mustn't give me away. Promise?" Marotta didn't give Thomas time to decide about promising, but went right on: "You're escaping in a basket, just like St. Paul."

"Now I know you're teasing me, Marotta."

"Cross my heart, I'm not," his sister replied. "You know how angry Pope Innocent is with Mother. But poor Mother—she would die rather than be excommunicated, and still she doesn't want anybody—even the servants—to think that she made a mistake in putting you in jail in the first place. So, she has decided that you have to escape—as soon as possible. And, Thomas, Mother is so anxious to see you again, and yet she is too proud to, after all she's done to you—and she's afraid it might look as if she were willing to let you go if she did see you—Oh, my poor head—it's all too much for me!" Marietta rocked her head in her hands.

"Too much for me, too, Marotta. But anyway it means I'll be free."

Later that day Father John was admitted to the tower. Theodora and Marotta and four husky men from the castle forge and armory followed him in. Father John was full of suppressed excitement. "Now, Thomas, do whatever they tell you. I'll be waiting down below." And he was gone.

"Okay, Brother Thomas, out to the parapet we go," said the chief smithy mysteriously. This seemed to be a great lark for everyone but Thomas.

"But—what about my books?" Thomas pointed to his table.

"We'll pack them and send them after you," said Theodora.

"Yes, you're enough load for one basket!" Marotta added.

"But—what about Mother—can't I even see her before I— ?"

"That would ruin everything, Thomas. You're escaing—understand?"

"Let's go, Brother Thomas," said the smithy. Thomas followed him out to the parapet. There he saw a huge basket strung with heavy cables, and at last he understood what Marotta had been talking about that morning. He gaped at the basket and then looked questioningly at the smithy.

"Get in and sit down, Master."

Thomas gingerly climbed in. The four husky men heaved the basket over the parapet and lowered it gently. There was nothing below but a narrow ledge of ground surrounding the castle's outer walls, then a sheer drop into the valley hundreds of feet below. On this narrow strip of grass Thomas saw the figure of Father John looking up and waving frantically. Thomas didn't like the view there; so he turned his face upward to the parapet, where the four men were hard at work at the ropes so that the law of gravity would not get out of control and dispatch the young Aquino into the next world. Neither the Dominicans nor the Aquinos would thank them for that.

Finally the basket touched ground—a perfect landing—and Thomas climbed out. It was the first time he had felt the earth under his sandals for more than a year. He threw another look up to the castle. The men were lifting the basket back up, but they stopped long enough to wave at the escapee. Now Theodora and Marotta had come to the parapet and were waving good-bye and throwing kisses to him. Thomas waved his arms widely to show them that he was all in one piece after his perpendicular journey. Then the two friars picked their way around the castle walls until they came to the road leading from the drawbridge.

Thomas was on his way once more.

Chapter 5: University of Paris

Vows

Thomas was looking forward to a nice peaceful time as a novice at Naples. It was going to be so wonderful, he thought, to live as a Dominican for once . . . to soak up the spirit of Father Dominic, to begin the climb to holiness together with all his new brothers under the firm but kindly discipline of Father John of San Juliano and the other friars he loved so much.

He was thinking about all this during that three-day hike back to Naples. But he had another shock waiting for him. Father John did not break the news until Thomas had caught his breath after his escape. Then he pounced on him.

"Well, Thomas, you're on the move again! Off to Paris with you—and long overdue, too. Master Albert's classes have already begun—"

"Master Albert of Cologne?" asked Thomas in wonder.

Father John nodded a "Yes."

"But I should never be worthy to study under him," Thomas protested. "I'd be much happier right here in Naples. And what about my novitiate?"

"Thomas, you have already put in your novitiate—and no Dominican ever had a tougher one. And as for your worthiness, well, from the record you made at the university here, and the studying you did in prison, it is clear to us that there isn't a better mind in all Italy. But you'll find plenty of competition in Paris! Besides, we've got to get you out of Naples. Your mother—"

"But Mother planned my escape from the tower. She couldn't be—"

"Your noble mother hasn't given up yet. As a matter of fact, she has written to our Holy Father again. And I have here a summons, transmitted to our master general in Rome, for you to appear at the papal court."

"Me? Appear before our Holy Father? Oh, Father John, why can't people just let me alone?" Thomas was really disturbed.

"Unfortunately, Thomas, you have become an international affair whether you like it or not. And I have a feeling that you are going to be getting publicity all your life. This must be your cross, Thomas—but if you just keep purifying your own mind and heart, you'll be all right. So, you will see His Holiness in Rome—on your way to Paris."

"But Father John, what if he won't let me go on to Paris?"

Father John smiled. "I don't think he will try to stop you. He is too good a friend of the friars for that!"

The next day Thomas made the three vows—the promise of poverty, chastity, and obedience—that every young person entering a religious order makes, right up to the present day.

The Pope's Questions

Pope Innocent IV was enjoying the visit of the Dominican master general, John the Teuton, and his young companion. He always enjoyed the Dominicans; they were so full of fire and zeal and ideas for converting and reforming Europe that it gave him new hope and courage just to hear them talk. But this visit was especially enjoyable, because he had been eager to have a look at this youth who was causing so much commotion in southern Europe just by joining the friars.

Of course the pope knew all about Thomas, for the friars in Rome kept him right up to date. But he never expected him to be a blond giant of a boy who towered over both of them, kept his eyes down, and said hardly a word. Whatever the Holy Father had expected, it wasn't this! Still, there was something about this boy, something he couldn't put a finger on—something innocent and childlike and at the same time wise and deep beyond his twenty years. And there was something magnificent in his ample, aristocratic build.

"Now, Brother Thomas, I'm going to ask you a few questions—with Master General John's permission," declared the pope, as he fussed with some important looking documents on his desk in the little office in the Lateran Palace (which was where the popes lived before Vatican City was built).

Father John bowed low. "Perhaps, Your Holiness, you prefer to speak with Thomas alone?"

"Not at all necessary, Father," said the pope, waving aside the suggestion with his hand. "Now, Thomas, it is reported to me that these crafty Dominicans have tricked you into joining their order because of your family's wealth and power, that they took advantage of a young student who was rather lonely in the big city—and in any case much too young to know his own mind—"

Thomas came to life. He raised his eyes and looked straight at the pope. "That is a lie, Your Holiness. All my life I was looking for something like the Order of Preachers, and I found it—all by myself—in Naples. If my family has been saying these things—" Thomas was out of breath.

"But doesn't it bother you to be one of this young upstart group of" (Pope Innocent cocked an eye at Father John) "—well, of beggars and riffraff like Father John here?"

Thomas was so excited that he forgot where he was. "You call our Father Dominic riffraff when he was from the Spanish nobility and a canon of the Church? Or Master Albert, or Father John? . . . Oh, please forgive me, Your Holiness. I forgot myself."

The pope seemed pleased. "That is just what I wanted to hear you say. You see, Thomas, I have the power to cancel the vows you made as a Dominican. You need not continue as a Dominican one moment longer, you will be perfectly free to—"

Thomas interrupted again. "Please, Your Holiness, with God's grace I shall continue as a Dominican as long as I live. I thought my mother would understand that by now."

"But doesn't it worry you that you are breaking her heart?"

"It makes me very sad, Your Holiness. I don't like to hurt anyone, but I couldn't go against my conscience any longer, and I pray every day that she will forgive me."

"She, forgive you?"

"Yes, Your Holiness. I am very grateful to my family for giving me an education and for giving me the chance to suffer something for Christ. I know now what it means to have a vocation—it means you have to suffer before you really can be sure. I know now that I want to be a good friar and a good priest, and I don't want anything else in life."

"Then I suppose my second proposition will have no interest for you. You know, Thomas, that Monte Cassino is looking for a new abbot, and it has been suggested that since Abbot Sinebald was a member of your family, and you spent your boyhood there and—"

"Oh, no, Your Holiness! Not that again! Oh, I love the Benedictines, but I could never be an abbot even if I were a Benedictine—and I'm a Dominican now. I could never change to another habit."

"You would not have to, Thomas. I can arrange it so that you may keep your Dominican Rule, wear your Dominican habit, and still be abbot of Monte Cassino. That way you could remain a friar and still save your family's honor. You know, things have not been going too well with the emperor's allies since you disgraced the family."

Thomas could not believe his ears. Why, he wondered, is it a disgrace to my family if one of us gives himself to God? Is God punishing my family for that? Is even the pope on my mother's side?

When he could find words, he said, "Please, Your Holiness, if the emperor is losing the war against you and the Church, it's good enough for him! And I don't see how I could help my family now, even if I did what my mother wants. I certainly don't want any honors for myself. I just want to work for our holy Faith."

"That is all I wanted to know, Thomas. You have made a good decision. And may I say, Father John, that I have never seen a purer, stronger vocation than that of Thomas here. Very few boys have had so much to give up, and so many obstacles to surmount. The Church needs boys like this as she never has before. This is the crisis of our life. Our enemies are closing in on all sides—but you know all this, Father John. So now I shall simply write to Countess Theodora of Aquin and inform her that her son refuses to change his mind and that she should stop annoying him in the future." He picked up his quill as if to write his letter right that minute, then laid it down again. "And I expect great things of you, Thomas," he added.

Santa Sabina

Thomas was taking a last look at the orange tree in the beautiful cloister courtyard of Santa Sabina. Father Dominic had planted that orange tree with his own two hands, and it had blossomed and grown through twenty-five years of Roman rains and Roman suns. (It is still alive today, nearly eight centuries later.)

Thomas felt very close to Father Dominic just now, and he hoped that Dominic was praying for his younger brother-son. Dominic knew what it was to start out on unknown ventures: he had walked unarmed right into the middle of the enemy's camp—and come out alive, with thousands of converts from the evil Albigensian heresy. Of course, Thomas was not going on any dangerous mission to the Tartars or Mongolians or even the heretics. He was only going to Paris to finish his studies for his theology degree and to prepare for the priesthood. But both Thomas and Dominic knew that there are many different sorts of dangers, different sorts of enemies, different sorts of heroes. Thomas might never die a martyr of blood, but he had long ago resolved to live a martyr to truth. And from all that the friars had told him in Rome and Naples, truth was having a very hard time of it in Paris.

Paris

As Thomas and Father John stood at the top of Sainte Geneviève hill and surveyed the city of Paris before they went down to the Convent of

Saint-Jacques they felt all the excitement of the great city tingling in their weary bones. Paris was something altogether new to Thomas. After quiet, battered old Rome and lazy, happy-go-lucky Naples, Paris was the "City of Letters and Mother of the Sciences, the noblest of all university cities."

People were thronging the street: students in their smocks (and some smuggling a baton of bread under the smock), peddlers with their wares, workmen hurrying to their construction jobs, realtors sizing up some old building they would soon be replacing with a tall apartment house, richly dressed citizens, priests and friars and university teachers—and always a procession of thick-tongued, side-wheeled carts drawn by men or horses or oxen and filled with limestone, logs, iron nuggets, sand, and anything else that went into building a new church or monastery or hospital.

Paris was having a building boom. And even though the two friars were jostled on all sides, with some unkind words addressed to them for being in the way, they stood fascinated by what they saw. For they beheld the most beautiful cathedral in the world: Notre Dame (Our Lady) of Paris. Its creamy limestone walls glowed through the scaffolding in the late sunlight. Its two square towers shouted their way toward the heavens, and squadrons of tiny pinnacles marched around the roof. Its lofty choir seemed to float on its island, as graceful as a Mediterranean galleon.

Father John spoke first. "I have watched that cathedral going up for years and years now, Thomas. When our Father Dominic came to Paris in 1219 to see Queen Blanche about starting our priory, only the middle part—the nave—was up, and it had no roof or windows. Now look at it—and it's all due to the generous people, great and humble, who have given their precious jewels and the labor of their hands. And see what they've done with those arches. See how they point up to God? That's a new idea. When they began to build, it was going to be just like all the old Roman churches with their round arches. But now they've pointed the arches so that they seem to be praying. But come, Thomas, you'll have lots of time to inspect the cathedral. If we hurry we can just make compline. Listen to the bells all over the city! It will be our first compline with our own brothers in nearly two months!"

Thomas was thinking how splendid it was that the new head of the Dominican order and a celebrated preacher in his own right, as well as a member of a great French family, stuck to his prayers like the newest novice. He decided then and there that he would always put obedience to the Rule ahead of any other job he happened to be doing. He was wondering, too, if he couldn't make his own life a cathedral like Notre Dame, a work of art glorifying God in every part of his being.

First Class Friend

Thomas was almost late for his first class under the greatest teacher in Paris, Master Albert of Cologne. He had to discuss his courses with his superiors and answer many tricky questions before he would even be admitted. Of course, the Paris Dominicans knew all about Thomas and his record at Monte Cassino and Naples, but Father John had warned them not to "let on." He wanted them to find out for themselves whether Thomas was as smart as people thought he was.

Thomas, for his part, was so used to starting out all over among strangers that he didn't expect to be received as anybody special. Only he was very impatient to get into Master Albert's lecture hall before the great man began his discourse.

He stopped short when he got to the door of the auditorium. The huge hall was jammed with young men. Sitting close up around the platform was a sea of white-habited Dominicans from his own convent (they had arrived first, naturally), with a gray shore of young Franciscans circling around them. Farther back, students and teachers from the other colleges of the university huddled on their straw mats and appeared to be holding lively discussions. Some were dressed as young dandies, some had threadbare academic gowns barely hiding their shabby clothing, some had clerical robes, others the attire of important citizens. There was no room for Thomas anywhere, it seemed, and with all the excitement of waiting for Master Albert to appear, no one had noticed Thomas until he began to pick his way through the audience on the floor in order to stand at the back wall of the room.

Suddenly, as one man, a little knot of students looked up, just as Thomas was about to step over the legs attached to one of them.

"Oh-oh, do you see what I see?" said a mouth belonging to another.

"Look at the size of him! No wonder the friars have to beg—when they have to feed and clothe giants like that!" from another.

"Might be interesting to find out if he's human," volunteered a third student, as he thrust out his leg to trip the towering Thomas.

Just then an agile Franciscan appeared at Thomas's side and kicked the offending leg back under its owner again. It was all so quick that Thomas did not even see what had happened.

"What say we have a little fun with him next time we see him in town?" suggested the would-be tripper.

"Good idea—he'll have to go into town to hear Master Albert's next disputation—it's a quodlibet—a special one," chimed in another from the group.

Thomas did not hear any of this discussion in his concern to get to the back wall. Nor did he realize that he had been clearing a path for that same Franciscan who had prevented him from sprawling on top of several students. The tall Dominican and the slight Franciscan nodded and were about to speak when the racket of a thousand chattering voices suddenly gave way to complete silence. Master Albert had charged in and ascended his platform.

Here in person was the greatest man in the world (as everyone believed)—great in learning, great in holiness. Yet what a simple, honest, humble look he had, what merry eyes and bouncy gestures. He was all electric! And when he started speaking, everyone was spellbound, especially Thomas. For Master Albert was worked up today, and about something very dear to Thomas's heart. He was bearing down on those who taught that the body and soul are enemies rather than friends and that the body is evil. From there he moved on to his favorite theme, that just as body and soul are really united in man, so should Reason and Revelation, Science and Religion, also be united for the sake of divine Truth.

"Go look at those pointed arches in the cathedral of Our Lady," he cried. "The Christian faith is the keystone of the arch. Pointing up to it on one side is Revelation through the Holy Bible and Christian tradition. On the other side is our human reason, fed by our senses. We need both sides to support the keystone of divine Truth. We are not angels!" And he proved his point with illustrations from physics, chemistry, botany, geography, and many more sciences on which he was the greatest living authority.

At one point Albert invited questions while he paused to get his breath. One young dandy thought he would have some fun. "Father," he said, "you just stated that people could live in the Antipodes—on the other side of the world—as well as here, and that they probably do. How could you possibly believe that? Wouldn't they have to stand on their heads all the time?"

"Ach, how foolish can you get! Why, they would stand on their two feet just like you and me, because the world is round, and they would be held by the same force that keeps us from flying off into space. What's more, young man, there are people living on an immense island west of the great ocean [he was speaking of America] and I'd like to live long enough to meet them. And they won't be standing on their heads either!"

With that he resumed his lecture, and probably would have continued it for the rest of the day, except that the bells for sext (noon prayers) started booming from the Saint-Jacques tower, from Notre Dame, and from a hundred other belfries. Master Albert wound up his lecture and left the hall. The audience got to its feet and swarmed out. The small Franciscan hung back with the Dominican, who seemed to be in a trance. He pulled at Thomas's sleeve. "You're new here, aren't you, Brother? Well, let me warn you: keep your eyes and ears open. Some of these fellows from town have the idea of—well, initiating you into university life. I heard them discussing it. I was right behind you—"

Thomas, coming down from the heights, was startled at first. Then he said, "You are very kind, Brother, but I can't believe that they meant any harm."

"You don't know, Brother! I've been around here quite a while, and I assure you they can be vicious—especially when their victim is a friar. They don't like us at all."

"But surely the king" my kinsman Louis, Thomas thought to himself, "wouldn't let them go very far."

"Look, Brother, there are thousands of students in Paris—some say as many as 40,000. Nobody—not even King Louis—could keep them from demonstrating, even though he is friendly to both us Franciscans and Dominicans. Did you ever hear what he said one time—that if he could be divided in two, he would give one half to the Franciscans and one half to the Dominicans? Well, don't say I didn't warn you."

Thomas was grateful to his befriender. "Okay," he said, "I'll be on the alert. But did you say you have been here a long time?"

"Four years. I was a disciple of Alexander of Hales, who just died, you know. A pity you missed him. But since his death I've been studying under Master Albert—and Albert goes even further than Alexander in his faith in Aristotle. But I've got to dash now or I'll be late for sext. We'll be meeting soon again, though. But, er, Brother, what's your name, if you don't mind?"

"My name is Thomas."

"Thomas what?"

"Just Thomas. What's yours?"

"Bonaventure—just Bonaventure."

The two young men laughed and shook hands to seal what they both knew in their hearts would be a real friendship. They did not suspect that their friendship would be recounted as one of the most beautiful in all history, even though it lasted only a short time and barely survived the later controversies between their twin orders.

Figure 4   St. Albert the Great

Chapter 6: **Albert the Great**

The Dumb Ox

If they had had weekly quizzes or monthly tests or yearly examinations in those days, it wouldn't have taken Paris so long to find out about Thomas. The students, however, merely listened to lectures, made their own notes, and did their own studying until the time for their big "disputation." At the disputation all the heads of the university gathered to listen to the student's "thesis" to find out if he deserved to graduate, and fired all sorts of questions at him. So it was a long time before even Master Albert got interested in Thomas. Thomas seemed to everyone to be just a big overgrown boy who never spoke up, even when the students were permitted to ask questions after a lecture. His classmates very soon dubbed him "the dumb ox," not because they didn't like him (you couldn't dislike anyone who was always so gentle and courteous), but because boys—even boys studying to be Dominican priests and missioners—have to have someone to tease, and Thomas gave them every possible opportunity. In fact, most of the students, and perhaps some of his teachers, wondered why the Dominican order, which was founded to train men for an intellectual apostolate, even bothered keeping Thomas on. Only the master general and those who were guiding Thomas toward his spiritual goal, and maybe Bonaventure, knew better, and they kept their secret.

Thomas was now twenty-one years old. He was studying to be a priest. He knew how serious a vocation this was, and how hard any young man had to work on his character before he would be even a bit like the great priest Christ, whose body and blood he would one day be bringing down to the altar. Thomas had already made up his mind to be just like Christ, and you couldn't be like Him without giving up some of the frivolities of the world.

Besides, Thomas was very busy—too busy to be clever or sociable. He was busier than the other boys simply because he knew more than they did, and that meant that he knew how much more he had to learn. It took all his spare time to soak up and understand and make his own all the deep things he was learning from his teachers. In short, he was contemplating the truth, not just memorizing and rattling it off to impress his classmates or teachers.

All the same, it couldn't have been much fun, or very easy for him either, to bite his tongue when he was tempted to contradict some brother who he knew was mixing up truth and error, or to boast a little about the Aquino family, or to fight back when they called him stupid or slow or "the dumb ox." But then, Christ hadn't answered back either, when Annas and Caiphas and Pilate gave him a chance to defend himself, and Christ had lots more than Thomas to be proud about if he had wanted to.

Only once or twice in all his three years in Paris did Thomas ever stand up for himself. One time was when the students were at recreation in the big heated sitting room (*calefactorium*) after dinner on a wintry afternoon. Some of the students were playing chess, some backgammon or checkers; some were trying hard to absorb as much heat as possible from the huge fireplace, hoping they could keep warm until evening recreation if not longer; some were writing letters home at the big oak tables; some were conversing earnestly; some were just sitting and thinking; and some were leaning against the stone windowsills gazing out at the snow falling ever so gently in the courtyard. Suddenly one of these snow-watchers turned around and shouted, "Hey, Thomas, come here quickly; there's an ox flying in the sky!"

Thomas jumped to his feet, got to the window, searched the gray sky, but saw nothing but snow. By now everyone in the room was in on the fun, and laughing merrily at Thomas's expense.

"Poor old Thomas," said the same fellow, as soon as he could stop laughing enough to speak. "Is there any hope for you? How could you believe such a thing?"

"Brother Philip, I'd rather believe that an ox could fly than that a Dominican friar could tell a lie," was all he said. That did it. There wasn't a sound. Brother Philip felt very foolish. And several other brothers began to wonder whether Thomas believed in the flying ox—even for a minute. Maybe he was just pretending to be stupid all along. A little later, one of the brothers decided out of pity to help Thomas with his studies so that he wouldn't flunk when his examination came up. Brother Luke supposed, maybe, that if he could pound just a few elementary ideas into his thick skull, Thomas could get by. So he took Thomas aside and started explaining all about "universals," Peter the Lombard's philosophy, when suddenly he got stuck himself—hopelessly stuck. He floundered around and around and then looked at Thomas with a foolish expression on his face. Thomas felt very sorry for him. He saw how embarrassed he was, and how much he needed help. So he took his classmate's notes and explained to him patiently and clearly and simply what his friend hadn't understood.

Brother Luke was so astounded that he just stared bug-eyed, then he blurted out, "Brother Thomas, you knew it all the time!" Because of the way he said it, Thomas felt as if Brother Luke was accusing him of some big crime.

"I'm so sorry, Brother Luke. I didn't mean to hurt your feelings. It was only the truth I was interested in."

"Please don't apologize on top of it! I was just too surprised, that's all. But say, Brother Thomas, what would you say to coaching me a bit? I'm the one who needs the help—not you. If you have time—" He was actually pleading.

Thomas smiled his kindly smile and said, "I'd be glad to, Brother. On one condition: that you never breathe a word of it to anyone. Okay?"

"It's a deal, Brother Thomas!" And Brother Luke made a hasty getaway. When he was out in the cloister corridor he mopped his forehead and whistled, "Whew! What a man!"

Albert's Discovery

At last Master Albert himself found out the truth about "the dumb ox." It was in 1248, three years after Master General John had deposited Thomas at Paris, and almost time for Master Albert to return to Cologne to become regent of a brand new house of studies for the Dominican students in Germany. Master Albert was lecturing on a difficult subject—the divine names of God—and hoping that what he was saying made sense to at least a few of his brighter pupils (and he didn't include Thomas in that group). After all the students had trooped out of the hall, Master Albert gathered up his papers and started for the chapel. He was worried about his new assignment in Cologne; he was worried most of all because he needed someone to help organize his new school—some young friar who was really a scholar, or who at least understood what he was trying to do. So far he hadn't found the one he had in mind—and he would be leaving Paris in just a few weeks. Oh, there were plenty of smart, quick-minded young men, but he was looking for someone special. So he was on his way to the chapel for his daily prayer for this special person.

Absently, Master Albert noticed some sheets of paper on the stone floor. Without knowing why, he picked them up and put them in order. Some student's notes—and that student might need them very badly. He would try to find out whose they were. They had been trampled on and torn, and the writing could hardly be read at best, but Master Albert managed to find the first sheet. On the top he read, "Ave Maria," then "Thomas of Aquin." At first he was no longer interested. "The dumb ox"—what could he have to say about a lecture on the names of God? Then something made him go on reading. He read as he walked. He didn't go to chapel after all but straight to his cell. He sat down and read to the very end. He could hardly believe his eyes. How could the dunce of the Dominicans possibly have worked out such a fine outline? Maybe one of the brighter students had let Thomas copy his notes? No, decided Master Albert: Brother Thomas didn't look like the sort who would steal from anyone. Besides, these were not Master Albert's words but Thomas's original thoughts. Well, he would soon find out. Master Albert laid the papers on his desk and went to the chapel. He wondered if the plot that was cooking in his mind wouldn't be too cruel. The Holy Spirit would tell him.

The next day, when Master Albert charged into the lecture hall, he didn't launch right into his lecture as he usually did; instead, he roared out, as sternly as he knew how (for he was really a very jolly little man): "Brother Thomas will kindly come up to the front of the room." There was utter silence on all sides as poor Thomas got up off his straw mat and stood before his professor's reading stand. For once nobody laughed at Thomas; they felt sorry for him and, besides, they didn't know when it would be their turn.

From his platform, Master Albert studied Thomas for a moment and then picked up the sheaf of notes he had found in the corridor. He cleared his throat and then began: "Brother Thomas, these are your papers, I believe?"

Thomas recognized them in embarrassment and said, "Yes, Master Albert. I think I dropped them somewhere. But I didn't need them anymore." He held out his hand for them, as he expected Master Albert to return them.

"You didn't need them? Ah, but I do." Master Albert clutched them to his habit. "I am going to question you on your observations right here and now, and you are going to defend yourself." Then he turned to the class: "And this, gentlemen, will be Brother Thomas's first public disputation!" At this everybody roared with laughter and settled back to be entertained. This was going to be a good show.

Master Albert motioned for silence, and then started firing questions at Thomas—and they were questions based right on the notes on Thomas's papers. Thomas answered every objection with complete confidence but with great respect and courtesy. This went on for nearly two hours. He was winning every round. But Master Albert still had some aces up his white sleeves. He would trip up this youth yet!

But no—Thomas crushed his opponent with a brilliant answer. That was the climax. Master Albert dropped his role of objector and said, "Brother Thomas, you do not speak as one on the defensive, but as a master expounding the truth."

Again Thomas had that feeling that he was being accused of something bad; so he said, as simply and apologetically as he could, "I can see no other way of answering the objections."

At this point Master Albert turned to the crowded audience and thundered: "You call this man a dumb ox, but I tell you that the time will come when the bellowing of his doctrine will be so loud that it will be heard to the ends of the earth!" Then he turned to Thomas, who was standing there as confused and miserable as could be, and said, so that the whole room could hear him, "You will teach this class for the remainder of the school year." Then in a lower tone, "I shall see you in my study this afternoon after none." (None was the prayer said in mid-afternoon.) Then he left the hall.

The Dominican brothers and some of the Franciscans gathered around Thomas, full of admiration and congratulations. If he hadn't been so bulky they might have hoisted him on their shoulders and carried him around the university in triumph. Then the sext bells started ringing and the students scattered, all except one Franciscan. He waited until they were alone, then he seized Thomas by the arm and squeezed it hard.

"I knew it all the time. I knew you had it in you, Thomas."

"No, don't, please, Bonaventure. Don't say it. Here, I've tried so hard to be humble and—"

"Yes, I understand, Thomas. But there comes a time when we have to face facts—and what is humility anyway, but facing facts, knowing where we stand? Take it from me, Thomas—I'm at least four years older than you, and I've been around the university longer than you have, and I've seen everyone worth seeing, and I'm a pretty good judge of people. I believed in you from the start. And I'm sure there's no stopping you from now on. I just hope that when you get to the top and have all Paris at your feet, you'll still have a thought and a prayer for an old friend—"

"My first friend in Paris, Bonaventure. I can never forget how kind you were to me that first day—and all the walks and talks we've had these three years; but we're talking as though we were parting forever instead of just going to dinner!" They were both hurrying from the hall now. "We'll have many more years together, won't we?"

Bonaventure was at the street door now. He paused and said, "I wonder."

Going to Cologne

Thomas knocked timidly on the great man's door. After all, no mere student had ever been invited in before. If Master Albert wanted to see one of them, he would corner him in his own cell, or in one of the alcoves off the cloister, or in the library, anywhere but here. When Thomas heard a reassuring "Come in!" he stuck his head in first, not knowing what he would find besides Master Albert. At first he didn't even find him. But he did see a big worktable and a forest of tubes, bottles, retorts, and cages. Then he saw Master Albert, a little bit at a time, rising to his feet on the other side of the table. The great little man looked up and smiled a broad kindly smile at his visitor. "Well, Master Thomas!" he said. "How's your German? You're going to Cologne with me. Or, I should have said, 'How's your Greek?' Because we've got work to do, you and I, and—oh, but let me find you a place to sit down! Let's see now, where's that chair? I did have a chair—somewhere."

While Thomas gazed helplessly about the cluttered work-room-laboratory-cell, Master Albert started removing piles and piles of big books off an article of furniture that turned out to be the missing chair—a very straight, primitive chair at best. "You see why I don't entertain many callers here—can't ask them to sit down, even if they can stand the smells!"

Master Albert motioned to his guest to take the chair, while he climbed up on his stool and picked up a long glass rod and started stirring something in a test tube. Then he pointed the rod toward Thomas. "For three years I've been looking for you, or someone like you, young man. I don't know why you didn't make yourself known and save me all this trouble. But I've learned all I need to know about you in the last twenty-four hours—especially the last three!" Master Albert cocked an eye to see how Thomas was reacting. "Well, aren't you curious about those three hours? No? Well, I'll tell you anyway. I was discussing you with our Master General, Father Prior, and your Father Confessor. Seems there's been a big conspiracy of silence going on all this time—and if it hadn't been for those notes you dropped, I would never have been the wiser. But it's all out now. From now on, there'll be no more hiding your light under a bushel. You're going to be right out there in the front line fighting for all you're worth till the day you die.

Ach, what a speech! You haven't had a chance to get a word in edge-wise! Well, why are you smiling, my young friend?"

Thomas had been overcome by his reception, but now he found some words. "Please, Master Albert, I was only thinking of what a hard time I had at home to keep from getting mustered into the emperor's army like my brothers. And now, I have to start fighting after all."

"I understand, Thomas. But there are different kinds of fighting. The kind of fighting you're in for won't be anything like what you may be imagining. You are going to fight with book and pen and tongue—with your mind, Thomas. I know it doesn't sound heroic—nobody will be writing any Song of Roland about you—but what you are going to do for God and Mother Church and yes, truth, will make all this blood and thunder like nursery stuff. You are a champion already, Thomas. Henceforth, you will be the champion of truth. Does that appeal to you?"

Thomas still hadn't recovered from all the surprises that had happened since ten o'clock that morning, but he was beginning to glow with an excitement deep inside him. "Oh yes, Master Albert, that is why I became a Dominican," he said ecstatically.

"Good! And Thomas, one more thing. I'm getting on, you know, and I won't be around forever. Why, I must be at least forty-five! And I need someone to carry on where I leave off—someone who understands what I am trying to do and can do it a whole lot better than I can."

Thomas couldn't have his beloved master talk that way. "Don't say that, Master Albert," he pleaded. "Why, you are the greatest man in Paris—in all Europe. Everybody knows it. Even Friar Bacon would admit that. No one could do your work any better than you. Look at all the books you've written and the—"

Master Albert shook his head and smiled. "I have done what I could, Thomas. But I am a pioneer. The most a pioneer can do in one lifetime is open up the frontiers—like experimenting in science." Albert's gesture took in all the projects on his worktable. "But you—you will have to develop what I have scarcely begun, you will have to draw all these things together and fit them into a beautiful pattern—like the thousands of little pieces of glass they are putting into the windows of Notre Dame. God's world is so wonderful, Thomas, and men are fast destroying it with their terrible attacks on it. To think of what's happening right here in Paris, with half the teachers spreading the most hideous errors about God—right under our noses." Albert sighed at the thought of it. "There is no time to lose. So, you see why I need you, and I need you quickly! You will go with me to Cologne and we will work out our strategy there."

Figure 5   Thomas taught by St. Albert (Dumb Ox)

In Cologne

Earlier, when Albert had first put down roots in Cologne in 1240, he had designed a mini-studium, a tiny house on Stolkstrasse ample enough for himself and his scientific paraphernalia and one or two student-assistants. Now, the big Dominican study house in Paris was jammed so full of young men wanting to hear the friars' lectures and disputations—and often enough hoping to be received into the new order—that the Cologne community was ordered to take in the over-flow, though it had long since outgrown Albert's little cradle, and was itself about ready to hoist a NO VACANCY sign when Albert returned there in 1248 with his prize protégé beside him.

"Your arrival in Cologne coincides with the ground-breaking for our new Dom—oh, excuse me, that's our word for cathedral," Albert re-marked as he led Thomas to the convent doorway. "But we'll probably have to build again long before that Dom is ready for use if it's any-thing like Paris—"

"But if it's going to be as beautiful as Notre Dame, Master Albert . . ." put in Thomas, implying that works of art always take a lot of time.

"Oh, it will be beautiful all right. I gather that they're copying the Amiens Cathedral, instead of Paris's, and that's the tallest building in all Christendom."

"Well, just so long as they name it for Our Lady," Thomas reflected.

"I hope they will, Thomas, though there's talk of making it a shrine for the relics of the Magi."

As soon as the two hikers had been led to their cells, Master Albert became one of the busiest men in Cologne. He was forever being called upon to preach in the city, and although he scolded the people severely for their sinful ways, they came by the thousands to the church where he was to speak. He was also running all sorts of experiments in his (very private) laboratory, and between a poke at a snake in a cage, or a stir of the vile-smelling mixture boiling in a test tube, and a look at the stars if it was nighttime, he was adding page after page to his latest book.

He was also a very holy man who spent many hours on his knees before his Lord on the altar and did a lot of charitable deeds for others on the sly. Moreover, as regent of studies for the Cologne Dominicans, he also ended up being president of a university. Because the courses for the Dominican students were so popular, hundreds and maybe thousands of boys flocked to them just as they did in Paris, so that the friars had to turn their own school into a university for the whole town. Albert had to see to it that there were enough teachers to go around and that students were studying the right courses and were keeping out of mischief. But, on top of all that, Master Albert had a new project on his hands: Thomas of Aquin. And this, to him, was the most important project of all.

Thomas's cell at the studium was right next to Master Albert's, so that he could burst in on the young friar whenever he had an inspiration. He let Thomas work with him on his experiments and study his notes on them, and he told him in a whisper about some of his theories that he could not discuss with anyone else because they were so far ahead of their time that the people might get frightened. When Albert was away on business for the archbishop or his master general, he had Thomas teach his classes and even preach the sermons he was supposed to give. Most of all, he helped Thomas lay the foundation to be a a priest and a saint. Thomas would soon be a priest, and he was sure that once he had brought God Himself down to the altar in Mass, he would never want to do another thing but hide in the chapel on his knees in adoration.

"The world is your cloister, Thomas my son. You just can't keep everything to yourself when people need the Word of God so badly. But you have to have the light before you can spread it," he said. And later, when Thomas was writing his biggest book—an encyclopedia about God and man and the universe—and came to the place to explain about the different sorts of religious vocations, he remembered what Albert had said, and described what he and Albert and all Dominicans before and after them were doing: to contemplate the things of God and to give over to others the fruits of one's contemplation. (In Latin the motto is: *Contemplare et contemplata aliis tradere.*)

Certainly Thomas was the luckiest person alive to have a teacher like Albert. And Thomas showed his gratitude by being everything Albert expected him to be—and more. Of course Albert expected him to hit the books hard—Saint Augustine, the Church Fathers, Christian tradition, and especially Sacred Scripture, as well as what he could get his hands on of the Greeks like Aristotle and Plato. But he was also subbing for his Master during his frequent absences, and finding that he enjoyed delivering sermons and lectures so much that he was tempted to concentrate on that side of his Cologne apprenticeship. But after two years, in 1250, he turned out what proved to be a bestseller, a stunning little masterpiece he called *De Ente et Essentia* (On Being and Essence).

This was a concise explanation of the radical new metaphysics of being that Thomas was developing. It was dedicated to his advanced "friar advocates" at Saint-Jacques who were excitedly following their brother's teaching but were not ready for his new vocabulary; so he came to their rescue with what amounted to a sourcebook of definitions. Saint-Jacques had been the right place for him to experiment with such ideas, for ever since they had taken over this property (donated by a University admirer and named for the neighboring church of Saint James of Compostela at the start of the pilgrim route to Spain), the Dominicans had encouraged daring, original thinking among their community, including temporary residents like Albert the Great. But now, in Cologne, within earshot, if not sight, of the "great" man himself, Thomas didn't feel any too daring or original.

After Thomas hesitantly laid the manuscript on Albert's worktable and tried—but failed—to make himself invisible, his preceptor soon came and confronted him with the material. "Brother Thomas," he demanded to know, "what have you been up to behind my back? This is the work of a master—the foundation of a lifetime of philosophical wisdom!"

"Please, Master Albert," he pleaded, "I've been thinking about this ever since I started reading Saint Augustine before we left Paris. I felt that somehow we ought to rescue him from the clutches of Plato."

"Plato!" sputtered Albert.

"Well, maybe not Plato, but the Platonists," Thomas said, apologetically.

"But how can you mean *rescuing* Saint Augustine—the saint who gave our order our Rule and—"

"Yes, I know, and that Rule suits us just fine; but his understanding of the nature of God... you see, God is pure act, a dynamic force."

"Where are you getting these ideas?"

"Out of my head, Master Albert. And there's plenty more where they came from."

"So? Then I hereby commission you to write and write and write until you've used up all those ideas."

"Master Albert, I've only begun," Thomas replied, his radiant countenance belying the discomfiture he felt.

Ordination

Those three years in Germany would have been completely happy for Thomas except for one thing: his family. Thomas always loved his family, no matter what they did to him or, through their alliance with the wicked emperor, to the Holy Father and the Church. But some-times in this life people can't do anything to help those they love the most—except pray for them. Thomas prayed every day for his family, especially for his mother and his two brothers, because he knew how wrong it was for them to remain on the emperor's side when all he wanted was to stamp out the papacy.

His sisters didn't worry him: Adelasia, the oldest, whom Thomas hardly remembered, was happily married far away in Spain; Theodora had a growing family of little counts and countesses Marisco; and Marotta had lived and died a holy life as a Benedictine abbess. But his mother and the sons! Thomas wore out his knees for them. God must have heard his prayers—but in a strange and heartbreaking way. Countess Theodora changed her attitude and became a penitent. Then, Emperor Frederick died, and when his son Conrad took over and started a new war against the Church, the two sons—miracle of mira-cles!—went over to the pope's army. Tragically, Emperor Conrad cap-tured the castle of Aquino, tore it to the ground, and took the brothers as prisoners. Count Landolph the younger died in exile because he had championed the pope's cause, and Ronald was thrown into prison and starved to death.

All this happened while Thomas was in Cologne preparing under Master Albert to be a priest. Sometimes he wondered if he had done the right thing. Maybe if he had consented to be abbot of Monte Cassi-no, with all its feudal rights and vast lands, or to be a bishop with a lot of power and dignity, he might have been able to do something for his family. But what could even an abbot or a bishop do? Thomas had seen with his own eyes what had happened to the old abbey, and no mere bishop could stop the emperor who wanted to conquer the Church herself! At any rate, Thomas must surely have been heartbroken. But there was nothing he could do but go on the way he was and offer up his heartbreak as a sacrifice for the souls of his parents and brothers. He knew he would be a better priest just because of that heartbreak.

When the day came for his ordination, and then his first Mass, Thomas was ready. And no doubt those wonderful hymns to the Eu-charist that you and I have been singing at benediction ever since were already singing in his mind. Thomas had no parents there to give his first blessing to, no little nieces and nephews clustered about him on the great day, but Master Albert had served his Mass, and all sorts of good German folk from town mingled with the students and friars to tell them how glad they were for him. Thomas was hardly aware of them. He had received an answer to his life-long question: What is God? He had held Him in his two hands . . . in the Holy Eucharist.

Chapter 7: Master Thomas

Seculars vs. Friars

Young Father Thomas was sent back to Paris during the summer of 1252 to study for his final degree in theology so that he could teach to others the truths he had been working on at Cologne. Master Albert had quite a struggle about that; it was the rule that a student had to be at least thirty-five before he could earn this degree—and Thomas was only twenty-seven. But Master Albert was not going to let a little thing like that stop him in his plans for his favorite pupil. When a very distinguished Dominican who was now a Cardinal-legate in Germany, Hugh of St. Cher, came to Cologne on the pope's business, Master Albert buttonholed him and persuaded him to use his influence at the University of Paris. It wasn't long before Thomas was on his way to Paris again—on foot, of course. He got there in time for his first big battle.

In February 1253, the secular teachers at the university (those who were not monks or friars) had declared war on the new religious orders, the Dominicans and Franciscans. These new orders were getting entirely too popular at the university. They were growing by leaps and bounds, taking in scores of the best students at the university and even some of the greatest masters, and these masters took their students along with them when they changed into their white or gray habits, gave up all their wealth and honors, and moved into Dominican or Franciscan friaries. What's more, many of the secular professors were openly teaching their students—many of whom would be ordained priests—doctrines that were opposed to Christianity. And when the Dominicans and Franciscans argued with these secular men, they always defended the true teachings of Christianity, and that annoyed the seculars; they wanted more than anything to have the friars dismissed from the university faculty and run out of town. But they knew that they would have a hard time making that happen, because neither King Louis (who took a very personal interest in the university) nor the pope (who took a very personal interest in the state of Christianity) would stand for any nonsense.

Then they had an idea: the leader of the secular party, Master William of Saint-Amour (which means "Holy Love"), would write a pamphlet attacking the friars and proving from the Holy Bible, and the Church's history and dogma, that they had no right to exist, that they were leading wicked lives, that they were enemies of the faith and maybe not even Christian at all—which was all very strange coming from the very people who in fact were challenging the Church's teaching and the truths of Christianity. Perhaps they figured that if they attacked the friars first, the friars would not have a chance to defend themselves. As soon as William finished his pamphlet he rushed a copy to the king, and another to the pope who was living at Anagni in northern Italy at the time. When the pope read William's attack on the friars he could hardly believe his eyes. "Something is wrong somewhere," he muttered. Then he decided to command representatives from both sides, the seculars and the religious, to come to Anagni and have it out—in his presence.

Both sides picked their best men. The orders chose the two friends, Bonaventure and Thomas, and their great old teacher Master Albert, who just by luck happened to be in Paris at the time—three future saints who were also the three best minds in Europe. The begging friars set out by foot, choosing the shortest passes through the Alps; the seculars rode in style on horses and with escorts and carts. By some miracle, the friars got there first. Not wanting to waste time waiting for the seculars, Pope Alexander IV handed each friar a copy he had made of William's pamphlet and gave them about twenty-four hours to prepare their defense; they weren't even supposed to discuss it among themselves. That was the first they had seen of the attack.

The next day the three friars, two in white, one in gray, filed into the courtroom where the trial was to take place. The jury of the four cardinals in their official robes sat motionless and severe-looking. One of them was a Dominican, the same Cardinal Hugh who had got Thomas admitted to Paris, but he pretended he had never laid eyes on the three friars before; in fact, he was interested in seeing that justice was done, even if his own beloved order lost the trial. There were several young priests distributed around the room with pens. The Holy Father stepped in and everyone rose reverently. When they were all settled again, they waited silently for the seculars to turn up. They waited and waited and waited. Finally the Holy Father said:

"Very well, gentlemen, this was the day set for the hearing. If our three friars here could make it on foot, certainly there is no excuse for the other side's being late. We shall proceed with the hearing. Father Thomas Aquinas will speak first, if you please. Kindly address the jury."

Thomas came forward, majestic in his towering height, yet humble and simple in his manner, and bowed low to the Holy Father, then to the cardinals. Then he began his defense of the mendicant orders.

Calmly, charitably, yet with deadly argument, Thomas blasted away at the scurrilous pamphlet of William of Saint-Amour. There wasn't a sound; the listeners hardly breathed for fear they might miss a word; the pope and the cardinals leaned forward on their chairs as though they were watching a miracle. Master Albert kept fingering the big rosary that hung from his belt. Father Bonaventure just kept smiling, so proud and happy was he at the brilliance of his Dominican friend.

Thomas finished his speech, bowed again, and sat down. Without betraying a sign of emotion, the Holy Father said briskly, "Father Bonaventure will now take the floor."

Bonaventure must have earned his title "seraphic" already, because everyone thought he looked like some sort of angel when he appeared before them. When he gave his talk about the spirit of poverty that Saint Francis and his friars had preached, he spoke as angelically as he looked. It was more poetic than Thomas's talk, which dealt with facts and figures, but it did prove that the Franciscans and their cousins the Dominicans were leading anything but evil lives.

Then it was Albert's turn. Truth to tell, these pupils of his hadn't left him much to say, but he didn't mind. He was so proud of them both that he should have been just as glad if he hadn't been called on at all. So all he had to do was summarize what the two young priests had said and then sit down again.

Pope Alexander rose from his throne and said, "Thank you, gentlemen. You have presented your case very well indeed. I do not think we need wait any longer to hear the other side. We have all read William of Saint-Amour's attack and have heard the defense of the mendicant friars. The jury has all the evidence it needs. We shall meet again after none to hear the verdict. We shall all go now and have some lunch; I imagine the friars are pretty hungry after their hard work this morning. But not a word about what has been discussed in the trial." Then he led the procession out of the hall.

Everyone was respectful and silent as they followed the pope down to the dining room, but little Father Bonaventure couldn't help seizing big Father Thomas by the arm and whispering "Bravo, Thomas! You did it again!" Thomas leaned down and whispered back, "You weren't so bad yourself, Bonaventure."

Despite their relief that the trial was over, the three friars were on pins and needles when they returned that afternoon to hear the verdict. After all, if the jury decided against them, it would mean the end of the Franciscans and Dominicans—which was just what the seculars hoped would happen. And they simply couldn't bear to think of such a thing. They were praying as hard as they could. When the leader of the jury stood up in his splendid red robes, three hearts almost stopped beating.

"Your Holiness," he began solemnly, "we find the Friars Preachers and the Friars Minor innocent of all the accusations contained in this document by William of Saint-Amour. We recommend that this document be publicly burned, that its author be banished from the University of Paris, and that the members of the secular party be required to take an oath of loyalty to the Church."

When the men from the secular party turned up three days later, they didn't receive the welcome they expected. In fact, they were sorry they ever started the fight in the first place—all except William, who was as stubborn as ever and refused to take the oath. He returned to France to sulk and to plot his revenge on the friars. (His pamphlet was later burned in the square of Anagni on October 23, 1256, in the presence of the Holy Father.) The three friars left for Paris like three schoolboys on a holiday, but they almost didn't get there. They took a little boat from Italy in order to escape the fast-approaching winter snows (which would make it very hard to travel across the mountains by foot). As it came across the coast of Spain on its way north, the boat began to founder in the tumultuous waves and winds and the sailors and most of the passengers were sure they would be shipwrecked. But Albert and his two pupils were just as sure they wouldn't: after all, God couldn't let them die when He knew how much more work they had to do for His honor and the salvation of souls, now, could He? Nevertheless, they kept on praying. And sure enough, they all got to shore in one piece.

After a leisurely trip on the Seine River aboard a grain barge, the three friars set foot in Paris at a freight terminal just above Notre Dame. Although they had just come from a magnificent victory that changed the whole course of Church history (don't forget that if they had lost their battle, if the pope and cardinals had believed what William of Saint-Amour had written about them, there would be no teaching and preaching friars), they made their way through the crowds of peddlers and workmen without attracting a bit of attention. They were glad of that, too, because the first thing they wanted to do was pay a visit to the Blessed Sacrament and to thank Our Lady (it was her cathedral) for helping them during their trial and saving them from shipwreck.

Inside and out, the cathedral was still a-building. Here a group of men were working on the stained glass windows, there, hacking at granite blocks. But even with all the clutter of scaffolding and clatter of hammering, the beauty of the building—the lofty arches pointing to the heavens, the brilliant colors of the stained glass windows, and the wonderful carving of the stone and wood—made the travelers hold their breath. They made their way up to the altar and knelt in silent gratitude.

Then they started for home, over the bridge and up Sainte Geneviève hill. Bonaventure turned in at his friary halfway up, and Albert and Thomas continued upward to Saint-Jacques', full of their own thoughts and too weary to speak. Just as they entered the gate, Master Albert turned to Thomas and said, "You have saved the order, my lad. But our struggles are not over—no, they have hardly begun. I must return to Cologne tomorrow, but you will go on and do great things. You may have to fight all alone, but do not be afraid. Our Lord said, 'Behold, I am with you all days.' And I have arranged with Father Prior to put at your disposal a very good brother from your country. He will be your secretary. You are going to be very busy from now on!"

Reginald of Piperno

At first Thomas hadn't quite understood what Master Albert was getting at. He was secretly hoping that now he could settle down to a peaceful life of lecturing and writing and, especially, praying. There were so many things he wanted to pray for—for purity, for light and guidance, for saying Mass worthily—that he had to start composing his own prayers to get it all in. He soon realized, however, what Master Albert had meant. Although nobody dared to attack the friars again for a while after what had happened, their enemies went right on teaching the same errors.

Some of them were saying that human nature was the very same thing as the divinity of God—and that is blasphemy, of course. Others were saying that there were two equal gods: one of good, and one of evil; and since the god of evil was responsible for the world and human nature, the only way to defeat the god of evil was to do away with marriage and the birth of children, or else to commit suicide by starving to death—and this was the vicious heresy that Saint Dominic had founded his order to fight against. It was vicious because it taught that everything in the world—the beautiful world that God had designed and made—was wicked. It was called the Albigensian heresy but was really only the Manichean heresy from centuries before under another name.

Additionally, some of the teachers were forcing their students to believe the philosophy of Persia and Arabia, which contained dangerous errors. And the worst of it was that they were calling it the philosophy of Aristotle, because they had translated Aristotle's books into their languages and had changed them all around to suit their own ideas. It wasn't Aristotle's thought they were using at all: they were only hiding behind Aristotle's name.

This was what Thomas discovered the day after he had returned to Paris. He was sitting at his desk before the window of his cell. He always loved the view of Île de France with its funny roofs and slender church spires and lovely skies. But tonight he was glumly thinking of how ugly a thing it was to deceive people—and that is what the Persians and Arabians were doing, and that's what the Paris professors were doing too. But what could he do to stop it? There wasn't even a correct text of Aristotle's writings to prove that the old Greek was not to blame.

Suddenly, there was a gentle tapping on his door, and Thomas said "Come in," almost automatically. He was too deep in thought to wonder who it might be.

"Father Thomas?" called a cheerful voice. Then a cheerful face appeared around the door. And then, as Thomas smiled a welcome, the whole cheerful person of a young fellow Dominican came into the room. Thomas had been concentrating so hard that he wasn't quite prepared to receive a guest at this point, so while he was arranging his words, the cheerful voice began again. "Father Thomas, Father Prior sent me up to make myself useful to you. Master Albert said you were going to be needing a secretary, and they picked me because I have a quick and—er—readable hand."

Thomas was used to complaints about his handwriting: he wrote so fast, to keep up with his thoughts, that nobody except himself—and Master Albert—could make heads or tails of it. He invited his new secretary to come in and sit down. When the visitor found the extra little chair, Thomas said, "But you didn't tell me what to call you."

"Oh, I'm Father Reginald, from Piperno. I have been a priest in our province of Lombardy for five years. They gave me the name after the great Reginald of Orléans, and I'll be very happy if I can be the friend to you that Reginald of Orléans was to our Holy Father Dominic—"

"Come now, Father Reginald, I don't deserve such friendship. Father Dominic was a saint and is going to be canonized. And me—well, I have such a long way to go." Thomas stopped and seemed very sad. He looked out the window. He always felt discouraged when he thought of how far short he fell of being what he thought a saint should be—how impatient, how distracted, how proud he was. Then quickly he brightened again. He turned to Reginald. "But maybe we can help each other to become saints. Or at least you can help me to be one. Will you be my confessor, Reginald? I need so much help—spiritually, I mean."

"Oh, Thomas, I was sent to be your secretary, and to see that you get enough to eat and enough sleep, for I'm told that you forget everything when you are working. No one said anything about the—other . . . matter. I am only a simple priest, Thomas—"

"Only a simple priest? But that is what I want to be, and you can show me how."

"No, Thomas, you have great and important things to do and write and—"

"All the more reason, if that is true, Reginald. You see, the more one has to do in the world, the harder it is to remember that God is all we are to be interested in."

Reginald felt like dissolving. He hadn't expected this of the man Master Albert was telling everyone about—the man who had saved the order last winter in Anagni. In fact, he had been almost too frightened to come to Thomas's room at all. And now this man, who Master Albert said would soon be the light of the Church if he wasn't already, was asking him to hear his confession and give him spiritual direction! It was too much for Reginald. But he pulled himself together and said, in a businesslike voice, "Very well, Father Thomas, I shall hear your confession, on condition that you follow my instructions carefully and don't try skipping any meals or working all night when you should be sleeping! Now then, speaking of sleeping, have you any work for me tonight? You were writing when I came in, I see—"

"No, I was only trying to write something. Reginald, we've got to smash this new philosophy from the East. It's corrupting the whole church. Hundreds of young men come to Paris to study for the priesthood, and they go away priests believing the things they are taught. Oh, it's horrible! And this revival of Manichaeism—it's going to infect everyone if it isn't stopped soon. To think that people could say that our bodies and this lovely world are evil, and that they are not getting married and are killing themselves to escape from it—we've got to get an answer for that first, or there won't be any people left! But what is the answer? That's what I can't get. It just won't come." Thomas put his head in his hands in anguish.

Reginald stood up and patted the big Dominican's shoulder. "Thomas, fear not: it will come, if you give your mind a chance to work on it. I shall report tomorrow, and we can get down to work. But—before I forget it—Father Prior asked me to tell you that you have an important engagement tomorrow. You and he are dining with His Royal Highness King Louis at his palace. The king has heard about your big victory and is greatly pleased, and I'm supposed to see that you have your new habit on and all—"

Thomas raised his head. "But how can I waste time like that when I have so much work to do? The Manichees . . ." He groaned. "Couldn't someone else take my place?"

Reginald drew himself up and pretended to look sternly at his boss. "Thomas, I realize that you have a great deal to do, but more important than anything is your vow of obedience. There now: you see what a severe confessor I am! Prompt and unquestioning obedience—that's the idea. But don't worry, Thomas, maybe something good will come of this—maybe more than if you stayed home stewing over the Manichees."

"That Settles the Manichees"

Father Thomas and King Louis IX understood each other very well. Thomas knew that Louis was a king with the soul of a friar, and Louis knew that Thomas was a friar with enough royal blood in his veins to start an empire if he wanted. Royal banquets were a bore for them both. Louis was much happier when he had his kinsman Thomas alone with him in his study (which was more like a chapel) and they could talk freely about the problems of a king who was more interested in the Kingdom of God than in earthly kingdoms. And yet, thanks to Thomas's good advice, Louis managed to be both a saint and just about the best ruler in history, giving his country a rule of peace, justice, and prosperity. Thomas, too, enjoyed those private sessions, for they gave him just the kind of encouragement he needed in his lonely battle for truth on the campus.

But Thomas's triumph over the seculars called for something special—not just a cozy heart-to-heart in the king's private office. The whole royal court and city and nation must see how much the king thought of his Dominican cousin and what Thomas had done for the university and the Faith. What could be more appropriate than a banquet in his honor? The only trouble was that King Louis wasn't aware that Thomas was in the middle of a paper on the Manichees.

King Louis's banquets were always modest by comparison with the orgies some of his successors were to stage, and the king never sat down until he had fed beggars with his own hands. Even so, it was a brilliant affair, with the first ladies and gentlemen of the land dressed in their most elegant fineries. The royal chef and servitors outdid themselves to make this a meal to remember. The Dominican prior and his celebrated companion, in their black capes over white habits, would have been distinctly out of place if they hadn't been born to fine families themselves. Father Prior enjoyed the company, the muted music of the lute players, and the good food, which was a treat after the plain convent food. But every time he looked across the table to where Thomas was seated between two charming ladies-in-waiting to the queen, he forgot all about the cooking. Thomas was not eating; he was not chatting either, and he seemed a million miles away—with no Father Reginald to tug at his sleeve and bring him back to earth. Father Prior prayed fervently that no one would notice.

Suddenly, between the main course and the dessert, the lute players ended their piece and at the same time, for some unknown reason, the chatting also ceased. Everyone had run out of ideas together, apparently! And then it happened. A white-sleeved arm was seen to go up in the air and a great clenched fist came down to the table with a crash. The table shivered, the goblets wobbled uncertainly, and a couple of ladies shrieked. "And that," thundered Thomas, "settles the Manichees!"

Father Prior jumped up, beside himself with horror. "Father Thomas," he called across the table, "remember where you are!" Then he bowed apologetically to King Louis. "Please forgive this, Sire. Father Thomas has been working too hard and—"

King Louis sat there unperturbed and smiling. "There is nothing to forgive, Father Prior," he said calmly. And quickly he turned to Joinville, his seneschal, and said, "Go get our secretaries at once, before Father Thomas forgets. This may be the most important moment in all our lives. It may be the salvation of the Church." Thomas seemed unaware of what had happened. He was still in the grip of his inspiration.

Just then Joinville returned with a couple of mystified scribes. They all bowed to the king and queen and awaited instructions. "Take Father Thomas to our study and write down everything he wants to say. Do not leave out a single word. That is all." Then he signaled to the musicians and the page boys to get back to business. The dessert appeared in record time, and everyone obligingly remembered something witty to say to a fellow guest. Amid the activity and the din, Thomas followed his "captors" out. Father Prior relaxed, and King Louis looked completely delighted with the whole episode. "We are highly honored and blessed that the light of the Church has chosen our humble home in which to shine," he declared.

Figure 6 St. Thomas and Reginald of Piperno at the court of King Louis

Chapter 8: A Second Term

An Outing with Students

Thomas bounded back to his cell to work a little more before it was time for a walk with the students. He could certainly have done without that interruption of his schedule, when he had so many jobs on the fire at once. On top of everything, he had just been notified that he was to represent the Paris province at a general chapter of the order—and that meant work. But he had promised his students that he would go with them today, and he wasn't going to let them down. They didn't have too many outings, with their stiff schedule. Besides, he never missed an opportunity to teach—and to learn; his students gave him plenty of chance for both. He was, after all, subregent of studies, and he took seriously his responsibility for the students' intellectual and spiritual development. These youths were the "beginners" for whom his greatest writing was shaping up in his mind.

They had decided to explore the right bank of the Seine and climb to the top of Montmartre—the hill on which the famous Sacre Coeur (Sacred Heart) Church now stands, though in those days there was an expanse of open fields between its summit and the middle of town where the new cathedral was going up. And it was miles from Saint-Jacques's, on the other side of the Seine valley. They tramped and tramped, talking as fast as they walked, observing every aspect of life that presented itself, referring everything to Father Thomas for comment.

Thomas began to feel very old (he was all of thirty-five) compared to these young men in their teens and twenties. There seemed to be no limit to their energy. But that was what responsibility did to a man, as they would soon enough find out for themselves. In any case, when they had reached the heights of Montmartre, they were all glad to throw themselves down on the grass to rest and rummage in the picnic basket their prior had sent with them. When they had demolished the last plum and peach and pear and were quietly enjoying the fine view of Paris before starting for home, Brother Augustine said dreamily, "What a beautiful city it is—if it only belonged to you, Father Thomas!"

Thomas probably thought this remark was pretty silly, but he always answered patiently and charitably, especially when the other person meant well. "And what should I do with the city of Paris?" he bantered. The half dozen brothers each had a different suggestion, from running the heretics out of the university to selling the city and building Dominican priories with the proceeds. Thomas rejected all the suggestions. "Right now," he said, "I'd rather have Saint Chrysostom's sermons on the Gospel of Saint Matthew than all the cities in the world."

Chapter of Valenciennes

The general chapter of 1259 in Valenciennes, which Thomas attended along with Master Albert, was one of the most important in the history of the Dominicans. It was called by Humbert of Romans, the master general. Raymond of Peñafort, an eminent canon lawyer who is now a great saint of the Church, was there too with two big problems on his mind. One of them was the problem of the Moors who had invaded Raymond's (and Dominic's) homeland Spain in such numbers that they all but swallowed up the Catholic faith and culture there. The other problem was to draw up an educational system for the whole order, which was growing so swiftly in so many different countries that it was difficult to maintain the same standards at every house of study.

For both reasons, Raymond was glad to have Thomas handy (in fact, he may well have planned it that way!). As for the Moorish question, after much discussion, Thomas was commissioned to write a book showing not only the errors of Moorish belief (that was only the negative side of it) but especially the reasons why the positive beliefs of Christianity were true. Pope Alexander was heartily in favor of this decision. What with teaching and preaching and getting his degree, Thomas took five years more to complete it (in 1264), but when it was finished, it was one of the greatest works of the human mind. Thomas called it the *Summa Contra Gentiles*, or a theological response to non-Christians, we might say. It became a bestseller, too, and was immediately translated into several foreign languages. With the help of this book, the Spanish Dominicans brought thousands and thousands of Moors into the Church.

But it was the second problem—that of planning a practical school system—that was the most fun for Thomas, because it brought him close together with Master Albert again. It was no longer a relation of teacher and pupil, but of two great masters and two future saints. It was probably the last time that the two were ever together—at least for any length of time—and we can just imagine the good talks they had while working on their new program of studies. The pair of them came up with a program, called a *ratio studiorum* (ground plan of studies), which was immediately adopted by all the Dominican houses no matter how far they were separated, and has been borrowed by every other order that has come into being since then.

That same year, 1259, Thomas finally won his master of theology degree from the University of Paris, and his Franciscan brother, Bonaventure, won his at the same time. The university officials deliberately kept the two friars waiting from year to year, although they knew perfectly well that Thomas and Bonaventure were the most brilliant theologians in Paris. The excuse they used was that Thomas hadn't reached thirty-five yet (but Bonaventure had!), when everyone knew that it was just out of revenge for the stinging defeat at Anagni. And their revenge wasn't finished yet.

Thomas became busier and busier, as invitations piled in to write on this or that topic and to preach all over Europe. He was also teaching his younger brethren and the university students who clamored for his help.

"Wow! That's a mighty hefty teaching load you've taken on," Reginald exclaimed as he looked over Thomas's schedule, "as though you had nothing better to do with your time. But you do like to teach, I know."

"I have nothing better to do, Reginald. And 'liking' is not good enough. It's a passion with me—if that's not too strong a word —because it's the perfect, ideal union of our contemplative and our active lives, which is what being a Dominican is all about."

Before Reginald had time to comment again, Thomas explained, "You see, the teacher has to make the truth he contemplates his own, and at the same time share it with others. And if he doesn't communicate it, he isn't really teaching. He teaches when he learns the art of looking at his topic through the eyes of his listeners, even innocent beginners, and that's not easy to do. He must be able to picture reality just as the beginners picture it, yet with the wisdom of a mature, disciplined mind. He must identify with the young, let them feel his love for them; yet they must realize they are being taught the truth and not just being entertained."

"But what's wrong with being entertained, Thomas?"

"Nothing, dear friend, but our job is to arrive at truth, not to amuse."

"And all this time you haven't said what truth is, Thomas. Can you define it in a few simple words?"

"Very well then. Simply, it's the way the intellect conforms with the thing it knows."

In spite of his passion for teaching, there were times when Thomas wanted just to live in quiet contemplation of God. Why couldn't they let him alone for a while? No, he told himself, that wouldn't be charitable. It wouldn't be right to cling selfishly to the sweetness of contemplation and be unwilling to sacrifice it for the salvation of others. He knew that if he made this sacrifice, God Himself would make up for the long prayers he couldn't squeeze in. And the Holy Spirit would reward him with inspirations that would make his work easier, if he kept living right in the presence of God, whatever he was doing.

Thomas's term of teaching at the university was supposed to have ended in 1259. The Dominicans had plenty of work for him to do all over Europe, and it wasn't fair to let the University of Paris monopolize him, especially after the way the religious orders had been treated at Paris. When the university officials realized that the Dominicans planned to transfer him, they were really alarmed. Things hadn't been going too well for the university; new universities springing up all over Europe were giving Paris plenty of competition, but not one of them had a star to compare with Thomas. He was the university. And now that he had been preaching the Lenten sermons—the biggest honor that could come to a priest in Paris—his public grew far beyond the university circle. All Paris was at his feet. So the Paris rectors sent a touching plea to the head of the Dominicans to renew his contract, at least for a few more years.

Master General Humbert of Romans gave in. Because Thomas had taken the vow of obedience, which (as Reginald reminded him) makes every command from headquarters the will of God for him, he had no thoughts on the matter at all. But none of them could foresee how soon the whole picture would be changed. In 1261, a new pope, Urban IV, ascended the throne, and this new pope was a Frenchman, Jacques Pantaleon, who knew all about Thomas. Almost his first act as pope was to wiggle a beckoning finger in Thomas's direction. He needed a theologian badly, and he knew where to go for one. *Roma locutus est*—"Rome has spoken," sighed Paris, sighed the Dominicans. Thus that same year Thomas and Reginald were on their way, trudging afoot with all the great unfinished manuscripts making up their luggage.

The Pope's Theologian

Thomas and Reginald sat facing each other across the square table that had supplanted the little scriptorium as Thomas's projects grew. Thomas was shuffling through the letters before him, and Reginald held his quill poised for action. But Reginald's brow was knotted up in a frown. Finally he said, "If you set aside all your important work every time someone wants you to clear up all his little doubts for him, you'll never finish anything. If I were you, I'd just chuck all those letters in the fire!"

"Reginald, I pray every day that I will always willingly give to others whatever I have that is good—as well as accept from others whatever they will give me. What becomes of charity if we hold back when we should help?"

"I know—but that one from Brother Gerard in Soissons—those six big questions (and pretty silly ones, if you ask me), and that one—thirty-six questions (no less!) from Venice, and these forty-two questions coming smack in the middle of High Mass on the Wednesday of Holy Week—that one about the workman and could he move his hand without heavenly intervention. And the master general himself bothering you. And now this young Brother John, still wet behind the ears—what a hurry he's in—has to know everything all at once—got to have all the shortcuts and expects you to give them to him," Reginald snorted feelingly.

"He is in a hurry, Reginald, and I think he really wants to know. We can't let these young boys down: youth is the hope of the world, and the hope of the order besides. Let's take Brother John first." Thomas pushed himself back and gazed at the ceiling, rocking on the hind legs of his chair.

"Brother John, most dear to me in Christ," he began. "Since . . . got all that, Reginald?" Reginald nodded.

". . . If you want to be admitted into the wine-cellar. Do you—"

Reginald looked up in surprise. "Wine-cellar, Thomas?"

"Just a figure of speech, Reginald. Like the king's storerooms in the Canticle of Canticles: symbol of the world of divine wisdom."

"I see what you mean, but I wonder if Brother John will."

"Let's give him the benefit of the doubt, Reginald. He might be discouraged if I said only that attaining wisdom is slow, hard work, and a very private, secret, lonely one, too. There now. We can tackle the rest tomorrow. But this will probably do more good than all the others together."

"I hope so, Thomas," Reginald said dubiously. "At least it ought to keep him quiet for a while!" He spread some drying powder on his paper, then blew on it and rose to go. "Now I'll go and get those books you wanted from the library. And when I return I shall expect you to be ready to dictate something really important. Brother John indeed! Hmmmph!"

Visitors

Thomas smiled after his fiery little secretary and obediently turned to the work in hand. But his thoughts kept wandering back to the sight of his retreating helper, and the steadfast, selfless devotion he lavished on his boss. Ever looking out for him . . . always at his service even if that meant being roused out of a sound—and, Thomas would have to concede, well-deserved—sleep to take down some midnight inspiration that wouldn't keep until morning. . . always joining in his doctrinal disputes with just the right reaction to clarify his thinking, and more important, in his vigils before the Sacred Eucharist.

He had once thought that he and Bonaventure would be friends for life, since they were united in the struggle to save their two orders. But what separated them—their serious differences on theological issues—proved to be more powerful than what they had in common. Now relations with Reginald were on a quite different, deeper level: never merely that of servant to master, or even disciple, scribe, confidant, infirmarian, fellow friar (that is, fraternal charity), but a really holy friendship. Without realizing it, they had arrived at a unity of spirit and mind—a supernatural, mystical gift of understanding—that he had thought only saints could enjoy; yet he and Reginald had received that gift together!

After that awesome intuition he got back to business. So what would he tackle first: the commentary on Saint Matthew, or the one on Peter Lombard's *Sentences*, or the "really important" one—the one that he hoped would provide the story of God that was churning in his mind since his effort on being and essence of a long decade ago. Yes, this was the one he must work on today. But not before he had prayed for help. He was stuck: he knew only that *being* is—. He cupped his hands over his face in wordless prayer.

A little later (was it minutes or hours? Thomas had no idea), Reginald rapped on the door and walked in, his arms piled high with rolls of vellum and massive books. Reginald's eyes took in the whole cell—nothing unusual about it. Thomas was writing so fast that he did not even hear Reginald come in. Reginald rushed to the dormer window, looked out: no—they couldn't have left that way—four flights down to the courtyard. Then he confronted his boss.

"Thomas, where are they?"

Thomas looked up in surprise. "Who?"

Reginald shot back, "Whoever was in here a moment ago. I've been waiting outside for half an hour till your visitors would leave, as I didn't want to interrupt. I only barged in because I thought maybe they were wasting your time. And now they've vanished—into thin air apparently!"

Thomas felt cornered. There was nothing to do but admit the truth. "Reginald, they did go—through thin air."

Reginald set down the books with trembling hands. He felt too weak to stand, so he sat down quickly. "You mean—"

Thomas was radiant. "There is nothing to fear, Reginald. Just two old friends who help me out whenever I pray the right way. Reginald—get your quills ready. We are going to work. I know now what I wanted to say: Being—the soul of metaphysics. Being—absolute, infinite being—that's God; finite, imperfect being—that's everything else. From this we understand what a cause is: the First Cause is God, we are all little secondary causes. But there must be a First Cause—see how it ties in with Master Albert's teaching on science? Now we have to work it out. Oh, Reginald, don't you see how it all goes together?"

"But who were those people you were talking to?"

"No, Reginald, don't ask me that."

Reginald was pleading. "Thomas, I only ask because I cannot guide your soul if I don't know."

"When you put it that way, I can't refuse you. But you must swear never in this life to tell a soul. Will you swear?"

"Never in your life will I give it away."

Thomas leaned down and whispered, "Well, then, it was Saint Peter and Saint Paul."

Reginald put his hand to his brow. "Oh," was all he could utter for a long moment. Then he resumed his role of secretary. "Thomas, I'm sorry but Father Librarian has no copy of Saint Chrysostom's sermons on Saint Matthew, and he doubts if there is one in all of France. But he said if you would ask King Louis he might get one copied for you when he goes abroad."

On his own, Reginald added that maybe the King would know somebody who knew enough Greek for the Aristotle job. "We needn't pester the King, Reginald," Thomas put in. "We have the very man in our order for the job—only I forgot about him because—" Just then there was a knock at the door, and Reginald took the message. "Thomas, your sister the Countess Marisco is in the parlor waiting to see you. Will you go down?"

"Theodora! I haven't seen her since she helped me escape. Oh, but Reginald, I can't stop now. I must put this down before I forget. You go, tell her I'll come in a little bit."

His Sister

Reginald bowed out as Thomas entered the parlor to greet his sister. Thomas was as serene as Reginald was nervous. One would think that it was Reginald who had just been entertaining Peter and Paul and was laboring to complete the foundation of the greatest philosophical system the world would ever know. Thomas and Theodora hugged and kissed each other, and then Theodora began to weep and laugh at the same time.

"Oh, Thomas, it's been such a long time and so much has happened." Thomas led her to her chair and then sat beside her, looking at her in wonder. She was a beautiful womanly woman, tall like her brother, yet somehow impulsive and shy as a young maiden.

"Now tell me every single thing about yourself and the family and what has become of all those poor servants at Roccasecca, and what you are doing in Paris, and—"

Theodora drew a deep breath and gave a lively report on the doings of the Mariscos: how Count Anthony was on a business trip to England and France, and now that the children were big enough to leave at the castle with their nurses ("Mother had turned over all her house servants to me before she died, so they weren't killed when the emperor destroyed Roccasecca"), he had taken his wife with him; and how Tommy was enrolled at Monte Cassino for school just like his uncle Thomas; and how angelic little Maria had been carried off by that dreadful measles. And—.

Theodora began to weep again at the thought of her little daughter. "Here I am, weeping like a child," she said as she dabbed at her eyes with a lacy handkerchief. "And me practically middle-aged! I guess things just got too much for me . . ."

"There's nothing wrong with weeping, Theodora. If it helps you, it's good. I'm going to put that in a book someday."

"You haven't changed a bit in all these years, Thomas," said his sister, brightening. "Remember those wonderful talks we had in your prison? You always understood. But I'm just glad it's you and not Anthony or the children seeing me now."

"I'm glad, too, Theodora. You have a duty to your family to be cheerful around the house, and to keep your husband faithful. Husbands have their worries, too, and—"

"Is that going in a book too?" Theodora broke in mischievously.

"If I can find a good place for it," Thomas bantered. "But seriously, Theodora, when things get too much for you, you ought to do what I tell my Dominican brothers to do when they get all knotted up with worries: just take a bath and a good long sleep. You'd be surprised at how well things take care of themselves—"

"You are a character, Thomas! And I was afraid you'd suggest something way over my head—just to punish me for fretting over my little problems. But I do have a big problem, too." Theodora lowered her voice almost to a whisper. "I want to be holy, and I don't know how."

"Just will it, Theodora."

"What did you say?"

"Will it! Turn your will to God, and your heart will follow." And Thomas spent the rest of their time together telling her all about the love of God and love of neighbor and how even a busy housewife could become a great saint.

When Theodora had to leave, promising to bring Anthony when his meeting broke up, she pulled a leather pouch out of her bag, wrapped Thomas's vast hand around it, and flew out the door to her attendants.

Thomas stood blankly with the pouch weighing down his hand. When he looked inside, he found a mass of solid gold coins. He rushed to his prior with it.

"Father Thomas, this is a very handsome gift. Since you have never asked for anything for yourself, I suggest you use this money for some of the books you need."

Thomas shook his head. "No, Father Prior. That's very good of you, but it would make me happier if you would give all the friars a real feast."

"We can do both, Thomas: a feast for the friars (how about on Saint Agnes's feast day?), and whatever books you need—"

"Moerbeke!" Thomas exclaimed excitedly.

"Moerbeke?" repeated the prior in mystification.

"Yes, William of Moerbeke, the world's best expert on the Greek language. We—Master Albert and I—finally tracked him down in Nicaea, where he's been living, and—"

"Doesn't sound like a Greek name to me, Thomas," the prior put in.

"He isn't Greek, Father. He's Flemish, from our Belgian province. He's mostly been doing scientific translating, like Archimedes' *Floating Bodies*. But when Master Albert and I saw what a fine job he did on his first Aristotle text, *The Politics*, we urged Pope Urban to bring him to Orvieto, since he's asked me to be there anyway to lay out the theology for reuniting the Greek and Latin Christians."

"But why is this ancient thinker so important to you—if a noddy may ask?"

"Because even the corrupt versions I've seen show how sound his principles are. Just think: he came close to discovering our divine Word through natural reason alone—"

"But what good is that, when we have Sacred Scripture, divine revelation, our faith—everything we need?"

"No, Father Prior, we still have to use our reason to back up our faith. Everything we know comes to us through our senses. In fact we couldn't even know of God's existence except through our knowledge of things, as you'll see when I've worked out my proofs for God's existence. Reason and faith are both gifts from God, but reason has rights of its own: it's our human tool for understanding reality. That's what I was getting at in *On Being and Essence*."

"Oh, yes, I recall what a stir that made, Thomas: you a mere stripling of age—was it twenty-four?—citing the *Metaphysics*, corrupt and all, at the top of the top page when you knew Aristotle was banned by the Church of God. So, you think that a better rendering of "the Philosopher"—as you call him, as though he were the only one—is going to change our image of that bad old world?"

"No, Father Prior, only the bad modern world where you and I happen to live. Because those texts were corrupted by enemies of our Church and our faith, and our Flemish-Greek Dominican is going to change all that."

"How so, Thomas?"

"Because he knows that it's next to impossible to translate word for word from one language to another. Every language has its own way of expressing ideas. You just can't simply substitute a Latin synonym for the original Greek word. You have to rewrite the whole thought in the Latin style or it won't be true to the Greek—or make any sense."

"You have my blessing, Thomas."

Chapter 9: Masterpieces

Greeks and Gentiles

Being theologian to a pope was no easy job, as Thomas was to find out the minute he set foot inside the Lateran Palace, where his new chief lived. Besides giving Pope Urban advice on every crisis that came up—and there was a crisis for every hour of the day, it seemed—Thomas was put to work on several new books.

Pope Urban wanted to have the Eastern (Greek) Christians reunited with the Western Christians and so did many of the Greeks—he regretted the break between them that occurred in 1054—so he asked Thomas to write a little book (*libellus*)—to be called simply *Contra Errores Graecorum*—that would do for those separated Christians what the other book he was writing—the *Summa Contra Gentiles* —would do for the Moors. At the same time, the Antioch Christians needed a book to give to the Saracen and Armenian heretics. Pope Urban, who had once been Patriarch of Jerusalem and knew all about these problems, passed their request on to Thomas. The pope also ordered him to complete his commentary on the four Gospels.

Figure 7   St. Thomas & St. Bonaventure

Sermons

Besides chatting with his scribe and all the writing, Thomas had become the most popular preacher in Italy, packing the churches wherever the papal court was held—in Rome or Orvieto or Viterbo. Every year that he was based in Rome he gave the Lenten sermons in the cathedral, an honor reserved for whoever was considered the greatest preacher that year.

Poor Reginald was run ragged trying to keep up with his master's dictation, seeing to it that Thomas took time out to eat and sleep, and forever fussing and fuming because Thomas was too busy to do anything about the "important" book he was supposed to be writing—the "beginners'" encyclopedia that would cover everything about God. Reginald grew sadder and thinner, and Thomas noticed it.

"Reginald," said Thomas, right in the middle of a sentence about the Trinity in his book for the Greeks, "do you feel all right? You don't seem to be yourself somehow."

"How could I be myself when I have to be five people and you have to be at least a dozen?" Reginald blurted out. "Thomas, if you don't let up, there'll be two more dead Dominicans—and we can't spare you!"

"I think that of the two of us, you are the one who can't be spared, Reginald," said Thomas, rubbing his cheek thoughtfully. "But what do you think can be done about our situation?"

"Go to the Holy Father with it, Thomas. Tell him that with four books under construction, you need four secretaries—one apiece. Tell him you have enough to do without being interrupted to settle every new scrape with the emperor and tell him you want an assistant papal theologian—and fast!"

"Ah, I've beat you there, Reginald. I've talked with Pope Urban already about that. Remember Father Annibaldo d'Annibaldi—"

"You mean Hannibaldus de Hannibaldus?—But just when he has been given your teaching post at the University of Paris?"

Thomas nodded. "He will be called Master of the Sacred Palace, and he's on his way here right now."

"That's wonderful," Reginald purred. "A real Roman noble—and almost a relative of yours, too. Didn't you tell me one time that your niece and his nephew were very happily married?"

"That's right, Reginald—but now about you. I'm afraid you will get sick if we don't find some help for you. You know, Francis of Assisi used to punish his body and call it 'Brother Ass' until it wore out before its time. It wasn't until Francis was dying that he saw his mistake, and then he called it 'Brother Body.' I'll talk to the Holy Father about you the next time I see him."

Thomas was as good as his word, but it was almost too late. Although Urban sent three more secretaries to help, Reginald had become so weary that when he was exposed to the germs that always plagued

Rome in the summer, he could not fight them off. Thomas prayed as he had never prayed in his life, but the Lord didn't seem to be listening. Then someone gave Thomas the idea of applying his relic of the sainted martyr Agnes to Reginald's chest. He should have thought of that himself, for Agnes had helped Thomas preserve his purity and had given her name to Dominic's convent for women in Bologna. Agnes apparently didn't mind, for on the instant the relic touched him, Brother Reginald rose from his cot perfectly well.

Bonaventure's Hat

Now that Reginald was his old self again, Thomas decided to take his own advice about taking care of Brother Body. Ever since Father Annibaldo d'Annibaldi had become Master of the Sacred Palace and a cardinal, he had been inviting Thomas to visit him at his family's palace in the suburbs of Rome. Thomas had always refused: too much work to do, he said. But now his friend the cardinal had invited him again, and Christmas was coming, and this time Thomas accepted. He dispatched Reginald to Piperno to be with his own folks.

The two friends had a pleasant time in the beautiful villa. They served each other's Masses, discussed their dreams for spreading Christian truth.

"You know, Thomas," said Cardinal Annibaldi one evening as they sat by the fire, "I feel ashamed to let our Holy Father make me a cardinal like this, when you just keep on refusing."

"You mustn't feel that way, Annibaldo. In your job you have to be just as high in rank as anybody you do business with. But if I were a cardinal it would be just a big nuisance to me. You can't be dignified when you're writing books. I don't know how Master Albert is going to manage being bishop of Ratisbon and writing books at the same time—not to mention the new Cardinal Bonaventure!"

"Speaking of your old friend Bonaventure," put in Annibaldo, "did I tell you what happened when our papal legates went to his monastery with his cardinal's hat?"

"I bet Bonaventure gave them an argument."

"Better than that—he gave them a lesson in humility and obedience. Seems they found him under the trees in the garden washing the community dishes. When the legates told him he was now a cardinal and presented him with his red hat, he calmly asked them to hang it on a tree until he had finished the dishes."

Rabbis of Rome

Just then a footman padded in to announce the arrival of some other Christmas guests—the two leading rabbis of Rome. Since coming to work in the papal court, the cardinal had gotten to know Rabbi Marcus and Rabbi Solomon very well, for the pope took special interest in their people. Cardinal Annibaldi had been watching for a chance to bring his Jewish friends together with Thomas.

After they were introduced all around, they settled down to spend Christmas Eve discussing the coming of the Savior, who, as Annibaldo and Thomas knew, was the Messiah promised in the Old Testament. Now Marcus and Solomon knew their Old Testament backward and forward; so all Thomas had to do was try to convince them that the God of their Scriptures sent His own Son—foretold by the prophet Isaiah—to complete the mission of the Jewish people. That was quite a job.

Before they knew it, it was midnight, and time for Mass in the palace chapel. All the Annibaldi servants and neighbors from the countryside were streaming in. The two Jewish rabbis sat reverently through the three Masses said by Thomas and the cardinal and didn't miss a word or gesture. Then everyone left the chapel for refreshments, and then on to their beds—everyone except Thomas.

Long after the big household was fast asleep, Thomas was still kneeling in the tiny sanctuary, praying for Marcus and Solomon. He knelt there till the dawn began to creep through the tall ilexes and cypresses, through the jewel-like chapel windows. Then he stole back to his room, as he didn't want anyone to discover his long vigil. If only God would give a birthday gift of faith to these two members of God's Son's race—the chosen race.

The next day, as Thomas was about to join in the feast-day fun, Cardinal Annibaldi caught him impatiently by the arm and whispered, "It worked!"

"What worked, Annibaldo?"

"Putting you in their path like that. Come to the chapel with me. We were only waiting for you."

When the two Dominicans stole into the chapel, they found Rabbi Marcus and Rabbi Solomon kneeling at the altar railing. Then and there Cardinal Annibaldo d'Annibaldi, assisted by Father Thomas Aquinas, received them into the Christian faith.

The news caused tremendous excitement in Rome, and Thomas became even more famous than his sermons had already made him. But

Thomas knew that it wasn't his arguments but his prayers that had brought the miracle of grace to the two rabbis.

Corpus Christi

After the Christmas feast day, Thomas went back to work with new zest. Now, instead of only Reginald, he had three more secretaries—one for each book. He dictated to them all at the same time, and for a while they made fine progress. Before long Thomas was summoned to another general chapter of the Dominicans, this one in London, England, in the summer of 1263.

Then he received bad news from Pope Urban. Emperor Manfred, Frederick's younger son, was attacking Rome again, trying to seize control of the Holy See, the Church's headquarters. Cardinal Annibaldi and his other advisers made Pope Urban flee to Orvieto, for though Urban was glad to die for his Church, he was needed to guide his people in this new crisis. And Pope Urban needed Father Thomas to guide him.

By the time Thomas and Reginald arrived at Orvieto (which was on the route to Rome from the north), the siege was almost over, and they could discuss another subject that was dear to both Thomas and the pope.

Thomas, we know, was especially devoted to the Holy Eucharist. When he celebrated Mass and could give God's Son back to God—and all the people of God with the Son—Thomas had a hard time to keep from dissolving in wonder and gratitude. It so happened that Pope Urban felt the same way. Moreover, it distressed both of them that the only day set aside to celebrate the birth of the Holy Eucharist was Holy Thursday, when the dark shadow of Good Friday hung over everything so that no one felt like celebrating. And especially at this time, when so many people were being influenced by the Manichean idea that physical, material things—even the Body of Christ in the Holy Eucharist—were evil, Thomas and Pope Urban felt that a special feast day outside of Lent should be created to honor the Body of Christ and win people back to the real heart of their religion.

Actually, Pope Urban had been thinking about this even longer than Thomas. Thomas was only five, and just starting to school at Monte Cassino, when a French cobbler's son named Jacques Pantaleon became an archdeacon of the diocese of Liège. Now in Liège, a Sister Juliana, a Cistercian nun who nursed in a leper hospital, was praying before the Holy Eucharist when Christ appeared to her and told her that a feast day should be set up to honor the Sacrament of the Altar.

Sister Juliana was questioned by several theologians: Hugh of St. Cher and three other Dominicans, Bishop Robert of Liège, and Archdeacon Jacques Pantaleon (the future Pope Urban IV). These great men agreed that Sister Juliana's experience was real, and they all wanted to start observing a feast of the Blessed Sacrament, or "Corpus Christi" (the Body of Christ). But when Bishop Robert died, many of the people in Liège rebelled against the new devotion (which shows how badly it was needed!) and drove Sister Juliana out of the country.

Archdeacon Jacques could do nothing about the situation, for just then he had been appointed Patriarch of Jerusalem, and his hands would be full there. But he never forgot his old dream of a feast of Corpus Christi. Now that he was pope, some thirty years later, his theologian Thomas of Aquino kept badgering him about it, and he could only say "We'll talk about it later, Thomas."

That "later" never seemed to come. If it wasn't the Moors conquering parts of Spain or the Christians in Greece parting company with the Holy See, or Arabians and Persians or Syrians disguising themselves as Christian teachers in the universities, it was Emperor Manfred trying to outdo his father (and how grateful Thomas was that his own brothers had died on the pope's side before this new persecution). Then . . .

"Well, Master Thomas, I'm always relieved when you are here with me, as I don't trust that Dominican Order of yours to let me have you forever. And just to make sure, I create you a cardinal here and now: Cardinal Thomas of Aquin, the pope's theologian."

"Please, Your Holiness, anything but that! I have not earned—"

"Nonsense, my friend. I have taken advantage of my exile in Orvieto to read the part of *The Golden Chain* you left with me. And it is superb, Thomas—the best thing ever written on Saint Matthew's Gospel, of that I'm sure."

"Then you should make the Holy Spirit a cardinal, Your Holiness," Thomas protested. "Please, please let me remain a simple friar—it's—it's my salvation."

"Don't be upset, Thomas," said the pope cheerfully. "I wouldn't force it upon you. It was the only way I could think of to tell you how I appreciate the wonderful work you are doing for divine truth. If there is any other way—"

"Yes, Your Holiness," Thomas put in excitedly, "there is another way—not of thanking me, but of doing something that would please me more than all the red hats in the world. You can institute that feast of Corpus Christi right now."

Pope Urban had not expected this. "Ah, Thomas," he said, wagging a finger, "you are a hard bargainer. So I have to institute a new feast of the Church, right in the middle of a crisis. Really, Thomas, it would be much simpler just to create a new cardinal."

"Your Holiness, the Church will always be in the middle of a crisis. Now is the time to strike back—on the spiritual front."

"I guess you're right, Thomas. Sometimes we depend too much on our own efforts instead of worshiping God, and then we wonder why we seem to get nowhere. But we'll have to get a new Mass composed, and"—Pope Urban was warming up to the subject—"a new set of prayers to go in the priests' breviary—but who's going to write all this?" Pope Urban looked sharply at Thomas. "I have it—you."

Thomas gulped in surprise, while Pope Urban went on. "You bargained with me. Now I bargain with you. You may have your new feast of Corpus Christi on condition that you compose the Mass and divine office and hymns—the whole liturgy."

"If that is the price, Your Holiness, I'll pay it. Or I'll try, at least."

The Texts

Thomas raced to his room in the pope's tiny villa. He had to tell Reginald straightaway.

Reginald was busy undoing Thomas's knapsack and putting his assorted writing projects in order. When Thomas burst in and breathlessly ordered him to clear the desks for this new assignment, his secretary looked reproachful as usual. "And now what becomes of your really important book? At this rate you will never even begin it!"

"Ah, Reginald, remember that little prayer you took down—'Lord, never let me begin my works before the proper time'? Well, the proper time for that book hasn't come yet. It is much more important that we honor the Blessed Sacrament of the Eucharist. Our Lord asked this Himself when He appeared to Sister Juliana—over thirty years ago."

Reginald relented. "All right, Master Thomas. Where do we start?"

"First, we go through the Old and New Testaments and find the best quotations referring to the Eucharist. That will be for the instructional part of the Mass. The hymns and prayers we'll have to think up ourselves. And oh, Reginald, they have to be right." And Thomas sank into his chair, trembling with fear.

"That should be easy for you, Thomas," Reginald said soothingly. "Your whole life is a hymn and prayer to the Blessed Sacrament."

Thomas didn't even hear his secretary's praise, as he was already deep in inspiration. And when he came to write the hymns he found that they almost miraculously wrote themselves, overflowing from his love of the Blessed Sacrament. And they were not just pious verses or difficult theology: they were literature, besides.

One of these Latin hymns, which begins *Pange, lingua* in the Latin, is still chanted whenever there is a procession of the Blessed Sacrament, and its two final stanzas, which begin with the words *Tantum ergo*, are always sung at Benediction. The other Eucharistic hymn everyone knows—*O salutaris Hostia*—is from another hymn Thomas wrote for the new feast. And the prayer that every priest now sings in English at Benediction is the entrance prayer from Thomas's Mass: "O God, we possess a lasting memorial of your passion in this wondrous sacrament. Grant that we may so venerate the mysteries of your body and blood that we may always feel within ourselves the effects of your redemption."

As soon as Pope Urban saw the finished product, he realized that he had made no mistake in giving Thomas the assignment. The new Mass, composed in 1264, has been recognized by liturgical experts ever since as the most beautiful liturgical text in the whole missal.

Pope Urban lost no time in sending out an announcement (or "papal bull") to make the feast of Corpus Christi official for the Church's calendar. It was the greatest achievement of his short term of office. And it's a fortunate thing that he didn't wait till "later." Later would have been too late. For Pope Urban was dead that same October.

Golden Chain

Among his many books, his book on the Gospels, which Thomas called *The Golden Chain* (Cataena Aurea), probably gave him the most pleasure of all his books, since he had memorized the whole Bible years ago while in "captivity" in his family's castle. Besides, his first degree in Paris was the *Baccalaureus Biblicus* (Bachelor of the Bible), which meant that all his lecturing and teaching during that period had to be based on his reading of Scripture. Even after he had graduated to *Magister in Sacra Pagina* (Master of the Sacred Page), it seemed to Reginald that Thomas was taking forever to cover those four Evangelists. Meanwhile, Thomas was organizing the curriculum at Santa Sabina and had managed to study the Greek Fathers' texts he had had translated. In 1267, he finished St. John's Gospel, the last of his commentaries, when he and his secretary were stationed at the papal court at Viterbo under Pope Clement IV, who had been elected two years earlier.

"Whew!" whistled Reginald. "Glad we've got that golden chain strung together at last."

"That's only a start, Brother. We still have to write about the Psalms, and that's very important because everyone in Holy Orders has to read the Divine Office every day and that's made up mostly of the Psalms, and the Song of Songs, and St. Paul's letters and—"

"And don't forget poor old Job—you ought to have some fun with him. But seriously, when will you ever start your book at this rate?"

"I wish I knew, Reginald. Every line in the Bible has to be scanned—"

"But why, Father?"

"Because it is the foundation of our faith, our religion. In fact, our Holy Father Dominic was called for good reason 'the Gospel man' by his successor Jordan. And our bright young scholars at Saint-Jacques have produced a reliable text to work from—and that text has to be reliable if young students are to learn to know the Lord through studying it. But, oh Reginald, there are the *Sentences* of Peter Lombard and all of Aristotle to comment on, now that we have him—the real Aristotle—in Latin, thanks to our friend William of Moerbeke."

"You mean the future Archbishop of Corinth," his secretary put in, with an accusing eye on the "simple friar" facing him.

"Right you are, Reginald, and we should be happy about our collaborator's honor."

"But Father, you're the one who's taken all the abuse for championing Aristotle when everyone else in Christendom –including some of our own brethren (like that English fellow Archbishop Kilwardby) and so-called friends like Bonaventure—considers him a dangerous perverter of truth.

"It's simply because the only Aristotle they know was smuggled into the West on the shoulders of the Syrians and Arabians and Persians," Thomas explained. "And don't forget—we have Master Albert on our side. But the real Aristotle, with all his great ideas about being—like matter-and-form, and act-and-potency—has made a Christian philosophy possible simply through our faculty of reason. In fact, this is his most beautiful achievement."

"So it's Christian philosophy versus Christian theology, Reason versus Revelation?"

Reginald bantered. "Take your choice—choose one or the other?"

"Not at all, Reginald. You choose both. It's a matter of reconciling the science of Aristotle—his art of thinking—with the Revelation of the Word of God. To think correctly is, in the main, to think like Aristotle."

The Summa of Theology

Finally, to Reginald's intense relief, he found himself taking down the words of Father Thomas that launched his greatest work: "Because the Doctor of Catholic Truth must teach not only the advanced student," he wrote, "we intend, in the present work, to impart the matters that pertain to the Christian religion in such a way as may befit the instruction of beginners."

As he searched for the best way to present such a massive subject for beginners, and tossing around—and rejecting—a number of approaches, after long prayer (Thomas never began composing anything until he had prayed for light) he hit upon a pattern that promised to be the best way to hold together the enormous amount of material he wanted to give his new pupils. It also sounded to Reginald like the shortest and the simplest. It would describe the movement from God the Maker to the world He made and all its human creatures—that would be the first part. Then the ascent of these creatures back to their maker—the second part. The third part would be about Christ, and show how His incarnation and His suffering redeemed mankind, and still redeem us through His sacraments.

"Sort of like the rhythm of a hymn, Master—or maybe like an architect's sketch for a new cathedral—an artistic device."

"Yes, Brother, that's the outline, the basic design." But before it left the designer's mind and entered his assistant's waiting pen, it had gathered into one vast compound of sources everything he knew or had mastered or pondered over the years from his first question at Monte Cassino ("What is God?") through his second stay at Paris—and that meant everything from Sacred Scripture to Plato to the Greek Fathers to St. Augustine to "the Philosopher" to the moderns of his day. "It's going to be a *summa* of theology—of biblical theology, for it all goes back to our Holy Bible, the Word of God." He looked in Reginald's direction.

"Another *summa*, Master? But hadn't we better define that word—there have been so many of them?"

"Right you are again, Brother. But rest assured, our project isn't going to be just another collection of disconnected facts. It will have an organic unity: everything will go together for the same goal—the sacred science of God, set forth so the new student will grasp it. And it will require all our know-how—our writing and teaching craft—to arrive at that goal. It's what I call the *ordo disciplinae*, the art and method of instructing the young."

And so, for the next five years or so, from about 1267 to 1272, wherever Thomas was located (for a while he was back in Paris, which meant discourses and disputations by the dozen), and whatever he was conferring about, he was driven by the urgency of the *summa* project he had taken on. But he could always retreat to a private little cell in his soul where he could concentrate on the difficulties he was trying to solve; most of all, he counted on his prayers for wisdom and peace.

Compendium of Theology

"I've been thinking, Father Thomas," hazarded his scribe, as they halted for a rest in their journeying. "You're making great progress with your book for beginners. But what about all the grown-ups out there who are hungry for truth and who've never had the chance (or the time) that your pupils have at Saint-Jacques or at the university? Maybe you could take a break from the *Summa* and dash off a sort of condensed manual?"

"You mean a compendium, Reginald? Why not?"

The mini "*summa*" (the *Compendium*) got off to a fine start. Like Reginald, Thomas was touched by the spiritual hunger he observed among the emerging class of working and professional people who flocked to the Dominican convent for the Sunday liturgy but hadn't "the leisure to study," as he put it in Chapter I; thus he planned to limit his presentation to "a brief compass for the sake of those whose time was taken up with the cares of daily life." Since man's salvation, he continued, depended on knowing the truth, Thomas organized that knowledge around the three greatest virtues, Faith, Hope, and Charity. After dedicating the work to "his dearest son, Reginald," with the counsel to "keep it continually before [his] eyes," Thomas launched into the first section (Faith), which opens on the unity of the Divine nature and the wonder of creation—a favorite topic of his. He was well into Part Two, on Hope, when he was plucked from Paris and found himself returning to Naples.

"What a bore!" Reginald moaned. "Couldn't they wait at least until the end of the term to tell you? I know how you must feel about cutting short your courses like that—and the *Compendium*, what's to become of that?"

The "they" Reginald had alluded to were the master general of the Order of Preachers, John of Vercelli, and the provincial of the Roman province. They had put heads together to schedule a joint chapter meeting at their church in Florence (Santa Maria Novella) over the Feast of Pentecost, which that year, 1272, fell on June 12. They had told Thomas to pack up his things and head down to Naples after the Florence meeting, to take over their convent there and make it go. They may have reckoned that Father Thomas could do with a change of scene, battle-scarred as he was from waging intellectual war on every side, and perhaps also that removing the chief target at the height of the tumult and turmoil would restore peace to Paris. Moreover—and this may have sparked their decision— Charles of Anjou, whom Pope Clement IV had crowned as king of Naples and Sicily in 1265, wanted back the star of the Dominican Order. His royal university at Naples had no theology department, but with Thomas installed at the priory next door his students could "do" theology there, at his expense and the friars' profit.

"No, dear friend," Thomas replied. "They couldn't wait. You know how hard it is to find a time when everyone can come together for a chapter; and what better time could they have found than the Feast of Pentecost?"

"But, Master, the *Compendium*?" Reginald felt very protective about this project, since it was dedicated to him. But how could he always "keep . . . before his eyes" its many chapters—256 of them so far, all stuffed with wisdom—if it never got finished!

"Not to worry, my friend. There will be time in Naples.

Chapter 10: "Welcome Home, Thomas!"

Return

"Welcome home, Thomas! How glad we are to see you again after—how many years is it now? Let's see . . . 1242 you came as a novice. That makes—good grief, I can't subtract any more—"

Old Father John of San Juliano was embarrassed, but Father Thomas d'Agni di Lentina, who had been prior at Naples then and had received young Thomas's vows, leaped to his rescue. "If this is 1272, that makes thirty years—and we've followed you in spirit every year of them!"

"Yes, and now we've got you home again," Father John added. "You belong to Naples, Thomas—and your faithful Reginald does too."

The two aged men were as overjoyed as children. Or perhaps grandfathers was more like it. They had been dashing young cavaliers when Father Dominic first touched them with his spirit. They were Thomas's wise teachers when he was a novice in Naples. And now they were enjoying, in Thomas, the intellectual and spiritual successes of the third generation of Dominicans.

Thomas was shocked at first to see his old teachers so bent and withered. But the love and peace that shone from their eyes, and the pride they took in their former students, turned his distress into joy. He hoped he could grow old so happily.

The two Dominicans from Rome did not bask in their welcome for very long. The University of Naples was growing faster than ever, both in enrollment and in scholarship, and the Dominicans, if they were going to keep pace with it, had to build up a first-rate house of studies like those at Paris or Oxford or Bologna. After all, they had had a convent there since 1231—only ten years after Dominic's death—and had dedicated it to their Holy Founder when he was canonized three years later. But that was nearly forty years ago, and their studium needed some fresh minds. With Thomas on their faculty, they would "have it made."

As for Reginald, he had pouted a bit at first about the move. The cardinal's hat he still dreamed of for Thomas seemed far away at the moment. But when Thomas pointed out that maybe now they could finish that important book, Reginald gave his blessing to the move. And Thomas was really glad to return to the Naples community so that he could enjoy a bit of peace and quiet after his hectic years in Paris and Rome and all over the lot with one pope after another. Besides, he still had this big writing job to do—the third part of his book about God—and you couldn't defend divine truth without living inside it, which is what contemplation means. So from mid-September of 1272 he kept to a busy but fairly orderly schedule of classes, public lectures, disputation directing, hard labor on the *Summa* and *Compendium*, and sermons at the priory church, especially those during the Lenten cycle of 1273, which drew hordes of people of every class, from the common folk and craftsman, to the merchants and lawyers, to the professors and academics. And a distinguished audience of outsiders came near to crowding out his regular students in the jam-packed Dominican lecture hall. After the daily crisis in Paris, it seemed easy. But only for a while.

Archbishop of Naples?

That "while" came to an end when one day he had a visit from a pair of papal messengers. When he bade the messengers farewell and returned to his study, he was pale, as though he had seen something worse than a ghost. He sank into his chair and buried his head in his hands.

"Father, what has happened? What did the legates tell you?"

Without looking up, Thomas held out a roll of vellum he had hidden in his wide sleeve. Reginald seized it, unrolled it, read it. "A papal brief!" he exclaimed. "The new pope doesn't waste any time, does he."

"Read it, Reginald."

"Archbishop of Naples . . . why, that's magnificent, Father Thomas—er, I mean Archbishop Thomas," Reginald purred. "And a papal brief is something you can't argue with." Reginald's prayers for a red hat for Thomas were answered at last, apparently.

"Yes, I can, Reginald," Thomas replied. "I shall go to Rome about it at once—or at least write him a strong letter."

"But why, Father? Pope Gregory X needs you. With this new war on his hands, he must have a good archbishop in Naples. And what reason can you possibly give for refusing?"

"The same one I gave Pope Urban: my salvation depends on my staying a simple friar. I can serve the new pope better the way I am, and that's what I shall tell him."

"I still don't see . . ."

Call to a Council

Reginald did later see, as the pope saw, that Thomas was right. The Naples studium was flourishing. Thomas returned to his own work, with Reginald's pen at the ready, when there was another interruption from on high. Pope Gregory had called an ecumenical council to take place the following May, in 1274, at Lyons in France. It was to deal primarily with Greek Christians who hoped to be reunited with the Latin Church. Gregory wanted the help of his outstanding theologian, and so he told Thomas to come running and to bring along the "little book" he had written back in 1263 for Urban IV. Thomas was never happy about that book, because the only sources available then were probably forgeries; and he began to dread another trek on foot when Reginald kept haunting him to wrap up his major work. But Reginald himself was daydreaming again—about that cardinal's hat his boss was sure to receive at Lyons.

As Thomas still had misgivings about his part in the Lyons venture, Reginald sought to comfort him by pointing out the great good the council would mean for the Church and the order—not to mention the Kingdom of Sicily. Everybody who was anybody was going to be there: at least 500 bishops and 60 abbots and about a thousand bigwigs like Master Albert, plus the Franciscans' number one man, Minister General Bonaventure, and even William of Moerbeke. And, Reginald added, "Of course they will make you a cardinal." When Thomas cut him short with "I can be of much more use to the order as I am," Reginald protested that he hadn't meant the honor would be for his advantage but for the good and glory of the whole order. But Thomas repeated more emphatically, "You may be quite sure that I shall go on exactly as I am."

Figure 8   St. Thomas and so much straw

Mystical Experiences

Reginald had certain misgivings too, but only for the sake of the *Summa*, which he felt was on a collision course with the interruptions caused by mystical experiences. These were taking place more often than ever.

The priory sacristan had seen Thomas raised three feet off the floor of Saint Nicholas Chapel while he was praying, and the wall crucifix said to Thomas, "You have spoken well of me, Thomas. What would you like me to give you in return?"

"Only yourself, my Lord," Thomas replied. That was on the feast of Saint Nicholas, the 6th of December, in 1273. From that day on, there was no more dictation. The *Summa* ended with the treatise on the sacrament of Penance.

"Father Thomas, what has happened? We're waiting for you to go on."

"No, Reginald, I cannot go on. Everything that I have ever written seems to me like so much straw compared to what I have seen and what has been revealed to me. The end of my labors has come."

After his initial shock, Reginald's first impulse was to shake his master's mind from the trance it was in and back to the *Summa* project, but he knew better than to persist. Thomas was not going to back down, nor would he reveal even to his confidant what he had seen or received in a revelation. This mystical experience was for real—not simply a physical reaction to overwork, as might have been suspected by fellow friars, some of whom were against the trip to Lyons altogether. Thomas meanwhile was going through the motions of community living, observing all the order's rules and even chatting pleasantly with his brethren at recreation as though nothing was amiss. But Reginald saw that he was truly living in another, otherworldly sphere that no one could reach. He was especially cordial toward Reginald, but in a vague, remote sort of way, as though not certain that he recognized him. This only added to the heartbreak his "son" and ally was feeling over his master's loss of creative power—as well as the dubious fate of the unfinished masterpieces they had labored over so long and hard. Worst of all was his fear that Father Thomas would be dying too soon to receive that "great dignity" in store for him at Lyons. It would be a race to the finish, and by now, Reginald couldn't wait till the end of January, when they would set out for France.

"Mental Exhaustion"

Their itinerary included a stop at Maenza to see his niece Francesca and her husband, the nephew of his friend Cardinal Annibaldi (just now away at Rome, where he represented King Charles of Sicily). By the time the travelers arrived at the castle, Thomas was so done-in that he hardly recognized his dear niece. She turned in alarm to Reginald and cried out, "What has happened to Father Thomas?"

"He needs to rest a bit, Lady Francesca, Reginald explained, as calmly as he could. "He's been like this—in a sort of trance—ever since the feast of Saint Nicholas when he banged his head on a bough that blew across our path."

"Then we'll get him right to bed," Francesca announced. "And have our doctor take a look—he's down with the servants right now, doing the annual checkup on all their children and the little ones from around the castle."

At this Thomas livened up enough to protest that he was content to sit by the window and enjoy the mountain vista outside—and he didn't need a doctor.

"Father Thomas, in my house you do as I say!" said Francesca with mock severity, as she sent her maid down to the lower level to collect Doctor John. He bounded up the long spiral stairway into the guest room, while Reginald and Francesca waited outside for his diagnosis. "I find nothing wrong with him that a good rest and some good food won't cure," he reported. "It's just maybe a touch of mental exhaustion. Probably been overdoing it for years?" He looked quizzically at the younger friar.

"That's true, Doctor," Reginald agreed. "He's been a kind of one-man industry as long as I've known him. But what's that 'mental exhaustion,' a new disease?"

"Oh," Doctor John answered a bit lamely, "that's what we medical men say when we don't have a better explanation—"

"Well, I have a better explanation," Reginald put in. "Master Thomas is dying of the love of God."

"That's a new one on me, Father. I'm out of my depth in such matters."

"So are we all, Doctor. It's a mystical thing—completely supernatural—but it can be a terrible strain on the body."

The doctor said, "I see," not seeing at all. "Well, back to my babies. That's more my speed."

Fresh Herring

After he had leapt back downstairs, Francesca entered and knelt beside her celebrated kinsman's chair. "Dear Father Thomas, you're going to be all right, but you must rest and eat everything in sight —doctor's orders."

"No, Lady Francesca," warned Reginald, who had followed her in. "He's hardly touched food since—well, Saint Nicholas Day."

"Then maybe I can tempt him . . . Dear Father, is there anything you'd enjoy eating and can't get at your convent?"

Thomas turned his gaze from the window and rested his hand on her pretty head. "Dear child, I only wish to get to Fossanuova before I die—"

"The monks are on their way to greet you right now," Francesca replied. "But you aren't going to die unless you refuse to eat."

After much urging Thomas admitted that he might enjoy some fresh herring such as he had sampled in Paris. Francesca consulted her chef about this delicacy, which she had savored on her wedding trip, and was informed that herrings were simply not to be had in the mountains of southern Italy. She had just turned and cried desperately to Reginald, "So what do we do now?" when her maid raced up the stairs and shouted, "There's been a miracle!" She almost collapsed of fright in her mistress's arms. Francesca and Reginald followed her back down to the scullery. The friendly fishmonger was still standing there like one struck dumb, and the chef and the kitchen maids had formed an unbelieving circle around him. Instead of the basket of sardines the mistress had ordered, what they saw was a basket of herrings.

For a long instant everyone stared and no one spoke. Then the chef observed solemnly of the neatly cut-up morsels, "These are of the finest quality and there're enough of them to feed a small army."

"Now to find a small army to come to our herring feast," Lady Francesca remarked. The castle doorman, descending to the kitchen area, overheard his mistress. "The 'army' is outside the gates right now, Lady Francesca," he announced, "and it doesn't look all that small, and it doesn't look warlike, either."

They turned out to be the peace-loving Cistercian monks, who had hiked in the cold the five miles from their abbey to greet their Dominican hero. Their ranks had been joined along the way by friars from the Dominican and Franciscan convents in the area. The commandant of the garrison—or more exactly, the herring host—beamed his pleasure at the scene: all his dear ones, plus all the loving monks and friars and the palace staff and as many country folk as had heard of the miracle, enjoying the herring treat and the merriment accompanying it. When Thomas himself was persuaded to try the miracle treat, he enjoyed it from first nibble to the last.

All in all, it was the best party Francesca had ever given, and she was certain that Thomas was already on the mend. But after another day or two, she saw that he was not improving, begging only to be taken to the abbey: "If the Lord is coming for me," he explained, "I had better be found in a religious house than among secular people, dear as they are to me."

Fossanuova

In another procession in the other direction—but a melancholy one this time—the Fossanuova monks, from the abbot down to the newest lay brother, formed a convoy around the Dominican friar they were leading on a donkey. Once inside the monastery he knew so well from many visits, he was heard by everyone to say to Reginald, "This is my rest for ever and ever . . ." After doing homage to the Blessed Sacrament, he was reverently installed in the guest quarters, where he was looked after with exceptional kindness. All the monks, even the most learned and holy ones, competed with one another to wait on him, even chopping wood for his fireplace and lugging the logs back on their shoulders rather than on their donkeys. In return they shared in the riches of his tireless mind as well as the example of his patience in suffering; and in their boundless generosity shared both with the Dominicans who were standing by, praying for a miracle.

As the "simple friar" and loyal son of the Church he wanted to be, he insisted upon taking every step in the liturgy of "preparing his soul" even to a general confession (over his whole life). Upon hearing it, Reginald ran from the room in something like terror, for as he described it, he had heard the confession of a five-year-old child.

When the end drew near, Thomas was helped from his bed and laid on the floor (after the example of his brother Saint Dominic) to receive the sacred host, brought by the abbot himself at the head of the whole community. "I receive thee, the viaticum of my pilgrimage," he prayed aloud. "Thee have I preached. Thee have I taught. Against thee I have never spoken. If I have held anything which is untrue, I subject it to the Holy Church, in whose obedience I now pass from this life."

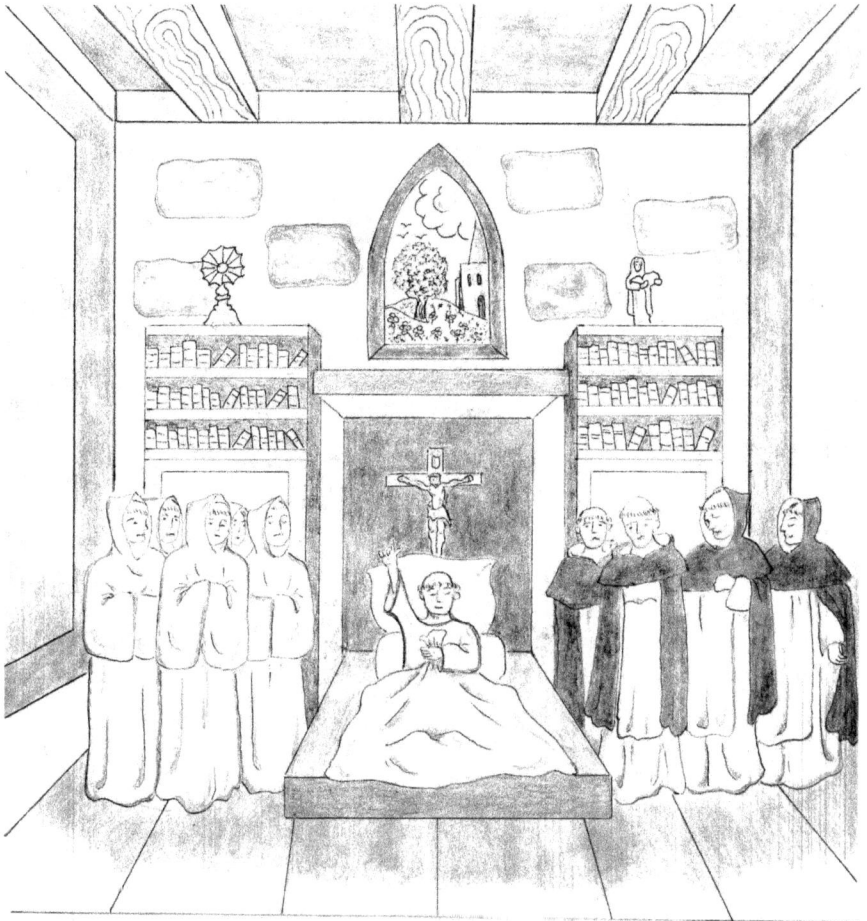

Figure 9   Death of St. Thomas

His Death

At that moment, which was early on March 7, in far-off Germany, his beloved mentor Master and Bishop Albert, in the midst of a community meal, suddenly began to weep. When his table mates looked at him in astonishment, he told them, "Father Thomas of Aquin is dead. This, God has revealed to me."

Lady Francesca was distraught when she heard the news, because as a layperson she could not enter the abbey cloister and tell Father Thomas her good-bye in person. So she begged the abbot at least to send the funeral procession the outside way from the cloister to the abbey church so that she and her friends from surrounding villas and villages could pay their respects. Her wish was granted: Francesca and the other noble ladies waved their farewells with one hand while stanching their tears with the other.

Inside the abbey church the Mass for the Dead was performed with the utmost devotion before a vast throng of monks, friars, diocesan churchmen, and as many distinguished citizens and common folk as could be squeezed into the noble old building. Then, with gracious charity (and perhaps an impulse of simple justice), Father Reginald was given the honor of delivering the funeral oration, since he was the most intimate link between Thomas and the world around him. But contrary to what some mourners may have expected, he did not dwell on his master's unmatched genius but told them instead, in emotion-filled words, of his prayerfulness, his humility, his mystical visitations, his charity, and his purity of heart. After the hearers' tears were dried, the body was laid to rest with great ceremony under the high altar in the sanctuary.

Then the commotion began. Miracles were being reported. People bringing paralytics and invalids, as well as mothers with newborns in their arms, were thronging to the church and clamoring for a chance to touch the holy man's remains. Hurriedly the monks hid the coffin in Saint Stephen's Chapel nearby, but after seven months had to return it to its original site as Thomas had ordered the prior in a dream. As they set about to do so, a most wonderful fragrance filled the chapel space and accompanied the procession into the main church. So instead of a Mass for the Dead (the second for Thomas) they had planned to celebrate, in a hurry they switched their chant books to a Mass in honor of the saints.

Although the Cistercians had hoped to keep their beloved Dominican's body forever, his own brethren felt it belonged to them by right, and Father Reginald was asked to draft a legal document to clear the way for its return. It took another century, but finally the body (still incorrupt) was transferred to the cathedral in Toulouse, the site of his order's beginnings.

The faculty of arts at the University of Paris—always the staunchest friends and supporters of Father Thomas—had less success than the Dominicans. Two years before his death, when they discovered that he had been pirated from Paris and seconded to Naples, they had begged the Dominican chiefs to change their minds and bounce him back to his university. To no avail, possibly because that would have ruined King Charles's plans for him. Then, when news of his death reached them, they asked in a warm affectionate letter not only for his last writings but, more important, for the honor of interring the body of their beloved colleague, "so good a priest, so kind a father, so outstanding a doctor."

For its part the theology faculty, where Thomas had occupied a Dominican chair with such incomparable brilliance, kept a stony silence in the direction of Fossanuova but instead seized the occasion of his death to intensify their attack, no longer on his person but on the image of the man and the principles which they attacked for years afterward. Indeed, the Archbishop of Paris, in league with the Archbishop of Canterbury (a Dominican yet!), had condemned a number of Thomas's propositions, a ban lifted years later when the pope intervened. Still, this persecution resulted in another miracle when Siger de Brabant, long a vigorous adversary of Thomas, changed his whole perspective and became just as vigorous a follower. And there probably were many others who accepted Thomas's teaching.

From then on, the story of Thomas took a different turn. No longer just the story of a man of matchless mind, it was also about the growth of his reputation and the flowering of his doctrine. He was called the Angelic Doctor, the Common (meaning universal) Doctor, Divus (meaning holy or godly) Thomas, Doctor of the Church, Patron of Catholic Schools. Throughout the centuries, down to Pope John Paul II in his encyclical *Fides et Ratio* (Faith and Reason) in 1998, Thomas has been hailed for his teaching as well as his holiness.

Unlikely Hero

But that is another story. Our story ends with an unlikely new hero, a young friar who could read his master's handwriting but whose career became a really privileged one when his master died. Reginald went on to complete the labor of their lives. He also set down his intimate and authentic memories of Thomas and interviewed others who had known him. He collected the materials into a kind of archive, just in case—but no, Reginald (he told himself), you know what happened to that red hat . . . .

Reginald may not have been around when the process of canonization got under way at the instigation of Pope John XXII (with some nudging from the Dominicans). But whether he saw with his own eyes or was following it from heaven, this process, which opened with a series of thorough inquiries, had a first-hand source in his documentation. Just about every witness at these interrogations could trace a link back to this source. Either Reginald had personally answered the witness's query about Thomas's holiness, or a later witness got his information from some witness who had questioned Reginald and then repeated that testimony to other questioners when they in turn had to take the stand—all under oath, of course. And when the canonization took place—a stupendous ceremony in Avignon on July 18, 1323 (even the King of Sicily made the trip)—Reginald would understand that such an event meant something better than the reddest of red hats—a new title for Father Thomas: **SAINT!**

Authors

Mary Ellen Evans

Mary Ellen Evans was born in Dubuque, Iowa, in 1912, and received an MA from the State University of Iowa. Most of her life was spent in New York City as an editor for Regnery, P.J. Kenedy, and Oxford University Press. Among her many projects was *The New Catholic Encyclopedia*.

She authored *The Christian Vision*, *The Spirit Is Mercy*, and the well-received *The Seed and the Glory*, a history of the life and times of Father Samuel Mazzuchelli, O.P.

A lay Dominican, she was devoted to St. Thomas Aquinas and his story. She cheerfully referred to herself as "the little old lady from Dubuque." She died in Dubuque in 2000.

Margaret Nichols

Margaret Nichols met the author through their shared interest in books for young readers. A classics major at Radcliffe College she later converted to Catholicism. She too was a writer, editor, and a poet, with work published in *Modern Haiku*; *Waterways: Poetry in the Mainstream*; *Salamander*; and *The Formalist*, among others.

It was her wish that young readers today might enjoy this story well before encountering the study of European history or of philosophy or theology.

Geoffrey Gneuhs

Geoffrey Gneuhs was a friend of the author for many years. Ordained a Dominican priest in 1977, he served as chaplain to the New York Catholic Worker, and preached the eulogy at Dorothy Day's funeral in 1980.

He has written for several journals and magazines, including *First Things*, *Commonweal*, *America*, and the *National Catholic Register*. He is editor of *The Legacy of Pope John Paul II* and a contributor to *A Revolution of the Heart: Essays on the Catholic Worker*.

A painter, he is a member of the Federation of Modern Artists and Sculptors. He maintains a studio in New York City.

Fr. Robert Staes, O.P., Illustrator

Robert Staes is a popular preacher, who has used his drawing pen to amplify his message. His illustrations of saints, and especially Dominican saints have enhanced a number of publications.   A hearty octogenarian, he continues to offer itinerant preaching from his Denver priory.

Index of Names